The Last King of Israel

The Last King of Israel

Lessons from Jesus's Final Ten Days

Michael Chung

WIPF & STOCK · Eugene, Oregon

THE LAST KING OF ISRAEL
Lessons From Jesus's Final Ten Days

Copyright © 2016 Michael Chung. All rights reserved. Except for brief quotations in critical publications or reviews, no part of this book may be reproduced in any manner without prior written permission from the publisher. Write: Permissions, Wipf and Stock Publishers, 199 W. 8th Ave., Suite 3, Eugene, OR 97401.

Wipf & Stock
An Imprint of Wipf and Stock Publishers
199 W. 8th Ave., Suite 3
Eugene, OR 97401

www.wipfandstock.com

PAPERBACK ISBN: 978-1-5326-0260-3
HARDCOVER ISBN: 978-1-5326-0262-7
EBOOK ISBN: 978-1-5326-0261-0

Manufactured in the U.S.A.   OCTOBER 24, 2016

Dedication

This book is dedicated to my PhD supervisor, Stephen Travis. It is because of your patient, detailed, thorough supervision that I was able to develop the academic skills necessary to do the research required for all I have published since our days studying together.

Robert Coleman, who was my professor during my MDiv studies, taught me what the priorities of life and ministry are. He has been faithfully and joyfully serving the Lord for over sixty years and has been a model of how I want my life to look like. I dedicate this book to these two men.

Contents

Introduction and Acknowledgments | ix

Chapter 1   *The Journey to Bethany* | 1

Chapter 2   *Jesus's Special Place* | 8

Chapter 3   *Rest* | 16

Chapter 4   *Martha's Metamorphosis* | 21

Chapter 5   *Meals* | 25

Chapter 6   *Dealing with Toxic People* | 30

Chapter 7   *Hail to the King* | 41

Chapter 8   *The Monday Temple Cleansing* | 49

Chapter 9   *Sanhedrin Stress and Story Time* | 58

Chapter 10   *A Beautiful Devotion and a Devastating Disgrace* | 63

Chapter 11   *A Special Season of Rest* | 71

Chapter 12   *Not the Last Supper* | 74

Chapter 13   *The Sovereign Savior* | 79

Chapter 14   *The Sorrowful Savior* | 84

Chapter 15   *The Submissive Savior* | 89

Chapter 16   *When Difficult People Assault* | 95

Chapter 17   *Preparation for Greatness* | 100

Chapter 18   *Innocent Persecution* | 105

Chapter 19   *Supreme Love* | 112

Chapter 20   *Good Friday through the Eyes of a Pharisee* | 119

Chapter 21   *Breaking the Sabbath for Personal Security* | 125

Contents

Chapter 22　Easter Sunday, the Hope of the World | 129

Chapter 23　Easter Evening Commission | 138

Appendix 1　A Bracketed Bethany Anointing | 143

Appendix 2　The Curse of the Fig Tree Scene in Mark 11:14 and Jewish Observances | 155

Bibliography | 165

Introduction and Acknowledgments

DURING THE EASTER SEASON 2014, I decided to blog on Holy Week. What I thought would be limited to an Easter-time exercise turned into a life-changing event. Having personally received much understanding, teaching, and encouragement, I decided to explore whether or not there was enough material for a book. After over one year of writing and research and two articles, I now have before you the unexpected fruit of that Easter holiday blessing. It not only changed my views and deepened my knowledge of the Easter season, it also began a journey of Gospels scholarship that I have dedicated the rest of my academic career to.

There are many people to thank, but I must first acknowledge one of my colleagues at Houston Baptist University, Dr. Jon Suter. Thank you for taking so much time to read the manuscript, offer suggestions, and paint my manuscript red. Many times I was humbled after you returned a chapter by how colored my pages looked. Your time is worth one hundred dollars an hour but I thank you that you only charged me lunch.

Wendy Leonard also worked diligently through my manuscript and offered many helpful edits, comments, and formatting. I sent many e-mails asking for her help and always received a quick response with helpful comments. I appreciate the time you took and the prayers you prayed for this project.

My colleague at Fuller Texas Andy Dearman also took time to read over portions of this manuscript. I also appreciate your friendship and support over the years.

Thanks to all at the Moody Library, on the campus of Houston Baptist University, like Katherine Diane Casebier and Dean Riley.

My old friend Judy Christians commented on my blog posts that planted a seed for the possibility of writing a book. It was your encouragements that help spark the idea that maybe these thoughts can be turned into a manuscript that could help others.

Much thanks goes to the students I have taught at Fuller Theological Seminary–Texas, Houston Baptist University, Houston Christian High

Introduction and Acknowledgments

School, and other institutions I have lectured at. It is you that give me my ministry purpose and it is for people like you that I write this book.

I also dedicate this book to my wife and sweetheart, Jodi Chung. If there was ever a proof there is a God, you outshine any theodicy. No way I could have ever been betrothed to you had God not existed.

The vision for this book is to be used both in academic and ecclesial settings. The ideal way to use this book in an ecclesial church setting would be to have the information read chapter by chapter then being reinforced homiletically and through community discussion. Homiletical outlines of every chapter are available and discussion questions are included at the end of every chapter.

Appendix 1 was originally published in 2015 in the *Bulletin for Biblical Research*, volume 25.3. Permission has been granted for its reproduction in this volume. Appendix 2, at the time of publication of this book, was still under peer review for publication considerations.

1

The Journey to Bethany

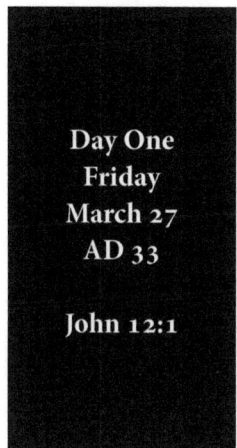

Day One
Friday
March 27
AD 33

John 12:1

We are all travelers in the wilderness of this world, and the best that we can find in our travels is an honest friend.

—ROBERT LOUIS STEVENSON

For the joy set before him he endured the cross, scorning its shame, and sat down at the right hand of the throne of God.

—HEBREWS 12:2

LIFE IS A JOURNEY. Its passage may transcend peaks of happiness, valleys of despair, waves of rejection, peaceful serenity, and interludes of rest. The voyage is long for some and short for others, but all take the journey. For Jesus, his final ten days, culminating in the resurrection, were a microcosm of his over thirty-three years of life,[1] bringing him to people and places that brought abundant pleasure and inflicted excruciating pain. For us today, the former should become regular destinations of the heart and the latter should be left far behind. Revisiting places and people that have brought joy in the past strengthens the soul to face the yet-to-come challenges of life's journey.

Jesus found a destination location for his heart in the village of Bethany. Before the Savior's journey to Jerusalem, where he would face cruelty, mental agony, false accusations, physical death, and rejection by his Father, he journeyed to Bethany to spend time with dear friends. The journey revitalized his body and soul before withstanding the suffering soon to be required of him. Redeeming humanity came at great cost, but with such a deep love, he chose to pay it.

---

1. Most scholars believe Jesus was born between 6–4 BC and died in AD 30 or AD 33. The dates used here are based on Köstenberger and Taylor, *Final Days*.

Passover was coming and the Scripture stipulated the Passover feast must be celebrated in Jerusalem (Deut 16:1–8). Although Jews from around the world had crowded the city, Jesus would have been able to find accommodations within the city limits[2] (e.g., he was able to find very suitable conditions to celebrate the "Last Supper" on short notice). Jesus was coming from Ephraim, possibly further away from Bethany and closer to Jerusalem. Despite the distance, Jesus chose to lodge with his friends in Bethany. He shows us that on the journey of life, it is important to spend time with those you care about. Despite being less convenient and out of the way, Jesus went to Bethany.

The way to Bethany traversed Jericho, the route someone from Jerusalem would travel if they were headed to the Dead Sea. In the Old Testament, Moses's successor, Joshua—which is the Hebrew form of Jesus—journeys through Jericho into the promise land.[3] Joshua's name means "Yahweh is salvation, rescuer, or deliverer" and God will use Joshua to deliver Israel out of wandering and settle into the promised land that God covenanted with Abraham almost seven hundred years before. Jesus journeys through Jericho (Mark 10:46; Matt 20:29; Luke 18:35; Mark 11:1) to Jerusalem and will rescue the world from iniquity.

It was Friday (John 12:1), ten days before the resurrection.[4] Jesus knew he was going to suffer and die (Matt 16:21–28; 20:17–19; Mark 8:31–33;

---

2. Though some would argue that his main reason for staying at Bethany would be due to overcrowding in Jerusalem during Passover. Given the business climate of the day, Passover would be one of the more lucrative times of the year for profit.

3. See Josh 3:1—6:27 and specifically 5:13—6:27. Jericho will be the first of many cities conquered by Joshua and Israel. On this issue of holy/divine war, see Thomas et al., *Holy War*.

4. There is disagreement among scholars as to the actual day to which John 12:1 is referring. Some hold to John 12:1 occurring on Saturday instead of Friday. Pate, *Writings of John*, 136, writes, "'Six days before Passover' no doubt refers to Saturday evening, if indeed Jesus was crucified on Friday (v. 1)." Keener, *Gospel of John*, 861, believes 12:1 also refers to Saturday evening. Keener accepts that in John's view, Passover begins on Friday evening rather than Thursday. Whitacre, *John*, 299, and Beasley-Murray, *John*, 208, also support Saturday. There are also some like Lindars, *Gospel of John*, 415, that suggest Sunday is a possibility. But Morris, *Gospel according to John*, 574–75, writes, "Six days before Passover could be the Sabbath, presuming that 14th Nisan that year fell on a Friday. Jesus may have arrived on the Friday after sunset, or alternatively not have traveled very far so as not to exceed the Sabbath's day journey." Carson, *Gospel according to John*, 427, advocates for 12:1 as a reference to Friday: "Six days before Passover most likely refers to the preceding Saturday, which began Friday evening. If Jesus arrived at Bethany that evening, just as Sabbath began, the 'dinner' that is described (v. 2) probably occurred on the Sabbath, the Saturday evening." Ridderbos, *Gospel according to John*, 412, describes

The Journey to Bethany

9:30–32; Luke 9:22–27; John 13–17). In one week, he would fulfill his mission (Jer 31:31–34; John 19:30). Luke described Jesus moving toward Jerusalem in order to fulfill his passion,[5] but on Friday, one week before Good Friday, Jesus moved toward Bethany to be filled by his friends.

Jesus's Sabbath Destination

Friendship is one key to happiness, and Jesus had close friends besides the disciples.[6] The narrative of the New Testament points to Bethany as a place where Jesus enjoyed meals, ministry, fellowship, and friends.[7] On this Friday, one week before his crucifixion, Jesus made the long journey to this place so dear to his heart (John 11:3, 5, 35–36), trying to reach the village of Bethany before sundown, the beginning of the Jewish Sabbath.

Sabbaths were designated days of rest. Just as God rested from his creation at the beginning of time (Gen 2:2–3), God incarnate—Jesus (John 1:1–5; 14)—would spend this Sabbath as Isaiah's Suffering Servant (Isa 52:13—53:12) with his close friends. Next Friday, he would journey from Gethsemane to Jerusalem and ultimately Golgotha, where he would spend that Sabbath resting in a tomb.[8]

---

the problem: "This time indication, however, gives no definite solution to the question of the day on which Jesus arrived in Bethany, since it is not certain whether the day of the Passover is included in the six days. Added to this is the question whether in John the day of Passover started on Friday evening . . . or a day earlier, the Synoptics clearly assert." Jesus would not be traveling on a Saturday so the reference to the meal in John 12:2 is likely Saturday but John 12:1 is likely Friday describing to the reader that Jesus will spend the Sabbath in Bethany. Holt-Lunstad, "Social Relationships."

5. The term *passion*, based on the Greek word πάσχειν (paschein) "to suffer," refers to Jesus's Triumphal Entry on Sunday till the Saturday before Easter. This work will refer to Easter Sunday as day ten.

6. One study by Holt-Lunstad, "Social Relationships and Mortality Risk," showed that "the quality and quantity of individuals' social relationships has been linked not only to mental health but also to both morbidity and mortality." See also Demir et al., *Friendship*, 860–72.

7. For more insight into the "Meal/Table Fellowship Motif," see Pao, *Waiters or Preachers*, 127–44; Smith, *Table Fellowship*, 613–38; Neyrey, *Ceremonies in Luke-Acts*, 361–87; Kelley, *Meals with Jesus*, 123–31; Seim, *Double Message*, 107–12; Koperski, *Women and Discipleship*, 517–44; Chester, *Meal with Jesus*; Blomberg, *Contagious Holiness*.

8. On the issue of "Journey Motif," see Green, *Luke*, 866. Luke focus on Jesus journeying to Jerusalem with the central pericope being Luke 9:51—19:44. The Greek word for Jerusalem appears twenty-seven times in Luke. See also Rosik, *Greek Motif*, 165–73, and Baban, *On the Road Encounters*, 113–26.

Jesus would not travel to Jerusalem this Friday to face Pilate. Instead, he would travel from Ephraim, near the wilderness (John 11:54), back to his beloved mountain village of Bethany (John 12:1).[9] This journey would be the last time Jesus ever sojourned in the wilderness. Next Friday, he would obediently complete the redemption journey and later return to be with his Father (Heb 9:23–24).

Notable Biblical Journeys

A long journey out of the way is nothing new to Jesus. Before he was born, Jesus, Joseph, and Mary journeyed almost one hundred miles from Nazareth to Bethlehem where Jesus would be born in a stable (Luke 2:1–7). Less than two years later, his family journeyed over four hundred miles from Bethlehem to Egypt to avoid Herod's reign of terror on male children two and under (Matt 2:13–15). Both long trips likely traversed wilderness territory. Today, Jesus travels through the wilderness for the last time.

Wilderness journeys are nothing new in the Bible (e.g., Moses and Elijah). In fact, Jesus himself had endured the wilderness before the Ephraim journey. After Jesus's baptism by John, that initiated his messianic ministry (Matt 3:13–17; Mark 1:9–11; Luke 3:21, 22; John 1:31–34), the Holy Spirit led the newly inaugurated King[10] into the wilderness where he would endure temptation by Satan and fast forty days (Matt 4:1–11; Luke 4:1–13). This journey was a typological parallel to Israel's forty years of wilderness wandering. However, while Israel failed God, Jesus would succeed. Today Jesus would again leave the wilderness—around the village of Ephraim—and be reunited with friends in Bethany en route to fulfill his passion. In the

---

9. The Mount of Olives is east of Jerusalem rising about 2,700 feet. From the highest point, Jerusalem and Herod's temple could be easily seen. In a correspondence with archeologist and Old Testament scholar J. Andrew Dearman, he commented on the Mount of Olives:
> The Mount of Olives is actually a ridge line located directly east of the temple mount and is part of the Judean mountains that comprise the landscape east of Jerusalem as the terrain eventually slopes down to the Jordan Valley. Bethany (currently a Palestinian village) is located east (ca. 1.5 miles) of the Mt. of Olives. In approaching Jerusalem from the Jordan Valley (as Jesus did), one turns west at Jericho (800 ft. below sea level) and goes up the hills to Jerusalem (2600 ft. above sea level). Bethany is one of the villages on the east side of Jerusalem that one could pass through on the way.

10. John frequently mentions Jesus as king: 1:49; 6:15; 12:13; 18:33, 37, 39; 19:3, 12, 14, 15, 19, 21. The Greek word for kingdom—βασιλεία—appears fifty-five times in Matthew's gospel alone.

Bible, as in life, to reach the mountaintop required an excursion through the wilderness.[11] If your current journey feels like a wilderness expedition where you feel dry and thirsty, tempted to grumble at your life's circumstances; consider that God may be preparing you for his work (Deut 8:1–5). He is allowing this wilderness for good (Rom 8:28). We will now look at other notable biblical journeys that foreshadow Calvary.

Abraham's Journey

There are prominent journeys featured in the Bible that foreshadow Jesus's final journey to the cross. Abraham made one in Genesis 22. He waited twenty-five years for his son Isaac's birth (Gen 12:1–3; Gen 21:1–7), God asked Abraham to sacrifice that son[12] (Gen 22:2). With heavy heart but in obedience to the God who had given him this son, Abraham embarked on a three-day journey to Mount Moriah. However, in the end, God did not require Abraham to kill his son. Instead, He provided a ram to sacrifice in Isaac's place.

Now, almost two thousand years later, eight days from now, Jesus would journey to a location very near the place where Abraham was called to slay his son. This time, however, there would be no ram to substitute for God's Son. Jesus was, is, and forever will be God's ram or Lamb of God for humanity.

King David's Journey

Almost one thousand years after Abraham was called to sacrifice Isaac on Mount Moriah and about a thousand years before Jesus would journey to Jerusalem, King David traveled to the very same location as Abraham (2 Sam 24:18–25; 1 Chron 21:18–26; 2 Chron 3:1).

---

11. Or in the case of Matt 17, sometimes after being on top of the mountain, a valley experience is nearby. After Jesus and three of his disciples Peter, James, and John leave the mountain after the transfiguration they encounter other disciples who are unable to exorcise a demon from a person suffering from an epileptic seizure. Jesus expresses his displeasure pointedly in Matt 17:17: "'O unbelieving and perverse generation,' Jesus replied, 'how long shall I stay with you? How long shall I put up with you? Bring the boy here to me.'"

12. Abraham had an earlier son Ishmael through Hagar but he was not the chosen one. Jesus would be born through the line of Isaac. See Gal 4:22–23.

In David's day, a census was taken (2 Sam 24; 1 Chron 21:1–17). The greatest Old Testament king of Israel had taken a census of his army during a time of peace. His actions were prideful, placing his faith in the size of his army instead of in the God he loved (2 Sam 24:1–17).

As punishment, God sent a three-day plague, from which seventy thousand people would die. Journeying to the threshing floor of Araunah, the same destination to which Abraham had traveled (2 Chron 3:1), David offered a burnt and fellowship offering on a self-constructed altar. God then relented from his punishments (2 Sam 24:25).[13]

In one week, Jesus would journey just outside the threshing floor of Araunah, but this time, God the Father would not relent. Jesus himself would be the sacrificial offering, and God would forsake his son just long enough to redeem the world. While Abraham saw God save one, and David saw God save thousands, Jesus would see God save all who believe (John 3:16).

Concluding Thoughts

With the journey motif so prominent in the Bible, it is not a surprise that the start of Jesus's final ten days begins with Jesus ending a journey. Friday, eight days before his crucifixion, the writer of John gives us a glimpse into the Savior's heart and life. With the Jewish leaders focused on Jerusalem and the Passover Feast, it was safe for Jesus to travel. Of all the places in the world the Savior could be during this crucial time, he chose Bethany.

Our life is also a journey filled with ups and downs, highs and lows, peaks and valleys. The journey of life is not an easy one, but having special places to go and special people to love will make the journey a little easier to travel. The next chapter will delve even more into why Bethany was a special place.

---

13. This would also be the site where Solomon will build the first temple.

The Journey to Bethany

Questions for Discussion and Personal Reflection

Jesus journeyed from Ephraim to Bethany in John 12:1. Think about your life's journey to this point. What are some of the best times? Worst times?

1. How did God use the difficult times in your life journey?
2. What lessons have you learned during this life journey?
3. Think about the three most significant people in your life. How did you meet them? Where did you meet them?
4. How are these times of blessing necessary for the soul?
5. At this point, would you say you are happy with your life's journey or not? If you are happy, how can you continue? If not, what can you do to change it?
6. Think of a time during your journey where you were most obedient to the Lord and a time where you were least; is there a correlation between obedience and fulfillment?
7. Meditate on Jesus's life journey. What would do you think were his ups and downs?

2

Jesus's Special Place

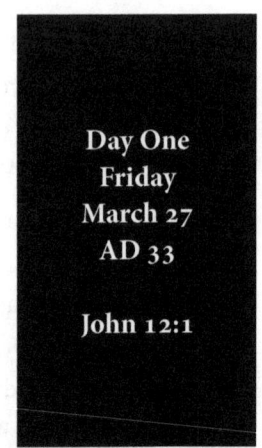

Day One
Friday
March 27
AD 33

It is good people who make good places.
—ANNA SEWELL

He went out to Bethany with the twelve.
—MARK 11:11

John 12:1

THE JOURNEY OF LIFE will lead us to heartfelt places. Some may have natural beauty, others will enjoy suitable climate, but most places become special because of the people who live there. For Jesus, one of his special places is a village called Bethany. Is there a place—city, shop, country, etc.—that occupies a special place in your heart? Are there dear friends/family that live there? For me, the city of Boston would be a special place. Every time I visit, my heart and soul are reinvigorated. It was in Boston that I had my first date with the young lady who would eventually be my wife; it was in Boston that I dropped to one knee and proposed to her. Jesus also had a special place beginning with a B called Bethany.

Why was Bethany so special? Clearly, the main reason was deep relationships with close friends: Mary, Martha, and Lazarus. The Lord of the Universe, creator of all things (John 1:1–5; Col 1:15–17) still made the journey to be with them. If God incarnate valued friendship, should not everyone?

Bethany is mentioned twelve times in the New Testament. Many believe the current location of the village of Bethany is a Muslim town with an Arabic name—Al-Eizariya/al-Azariya—which means "Place of Lazarus." Located on the southeastern slope of the Mount of Olives about two miles from Jerusalem.

Jesus's Special Place

Bethany: A Place of the Miraculous

If Jesus tried so hard to get to Bethany, what other aspects would make this place a destination where he wanted to spend his last days? Bethany was not just a place of ministry, but also a place of the miraculous, the site where he performed one of his great sign miracles showing he was Messiah. Lazarus had died. Four days after his death, Jesus arrived in Bethany (John 11:17).[1] Jewish people believe the soul remained in close proximity to the corpse for up to three days.[2] Arriving on day four would erase any hope of resuscitating Lazarus from the dead.[3] With Jesus, when all seems hopeless, God revives hope.

Jesus interacts with close friends, Lazarus's grieving sisters, Mary and Martha, telling them both to believe. The sisters are mourning and disappointed; they knew Jesus loved their brother and could heal him (John 11:32), but Jesus never appeared and, after four days, the sisters had lost all expectation that their brother would live again. Unknown to them, Jesus was preparing to restore in a way beyond all they can ask or think. The sisters were to be reunited with their brother on earth and not have to wait until heaven.

A prayer to the Father followed by an exclamation to his deceased friend, "Lazarus, come out," and just as the Lord had proclaimed, Lazarus came out (John 11:17–44).[4] The disappointments the sisters experienced and the mourning their souls were suffering have now been removed, the

---

1. Esler and Piper, *Lazarus, Mary and Martha*, 8, writes, "The geographical setting is prefigured in part in John 10:40–42, where Jesus and his disciples travel to the far side of the Jordan where John had previously baptized, meaning that Jesus is a long way from Bethany when Lazarus fall ill."

2. See Carson, *Gospel according to John*, 411.

3. Carson writes, "There are sources attesting the rabbinic belief that the soul hovers over the body of the deceased person for the first three days . . . but as soon as it sees . . . that decomposition has set in, it departs. . . . At that point death is irreversible" (ibid.).

4. Jesus resurrecting of Lazarus from the dead would be the last of the seven signs in the first part of John's Gospel often referred to as the book of signs (John 1:19—12:50). The other six "signs" in John are: Changing water into wine (2:1–11); Healing the royal official's son at Capernaum (4:46–54); Healing the paralytic at Bethesda (5:1–18); Feeding the 5,000 (6:5–14); Jesus's walk on water (6:16–24); Healing the man born blind (9:1–7). The Greek word for signs—shmei/on,—appears 17 times in the book of John, 16 of the occurrences are from ch. 2 through ch. 12 and does not appear until John 20:30. Byrne, *Lazarus*, 18–20, argues for only six signs and would remove Jesus walking on water as a sign because there is no human need present nor Jesus miraculously curing a human need.

very one they were hoping to come four days earlier had done what they knew he could do. Lazarus's sisters reminds us that God has his own best timing to do things, and our timing usually does not coincide. His brings most glory to his name.

Bethany's Miracle Brings Danger

Certainly a miracle like raising someone from the dead would lead every man, woman, and child who witnessed or heard about this resurrection to faith. It did not! Though many believed, the religious leaders—the chief priests and the Pharisees—two of the bodies that would know Scriptures the best, called a meeting of the Sanhedrin, the high court of the Jews (John 11:45–47).[5] Instead of worship, Jesus's miracle produced war. They wanted Jesus dead. The Romans gave the Sanhedrin great authority but the highest court of the Jews was unable to administer a death penalty.[6] These erudite religious leaders of the day did not bow down and worship Jesus as the Messiah, but feared that people would follow him and prompt Rome to remove their temple and nation, which ironically, Rome eventually did in AD 70 (John 11:48).[7]

When people feel threatened, they become emotional, afraid, and irrational. The Jewish religious leaders—the ones who should have known Messiah had arrived—were the very ones who were threatened. They were blinded by fear, stubborn in heart, and valuing their own personal empires of prominence over Jesus's kingdom.[8] They could not see that Messiah had come and their stubbornness was witnessed throughout the last ten days.

---

5. Pate, *Writings of John*, 524, writes the Sanhedrin is "the political ruling body over Israel during Jesus's day. It comprised 71 members, including the high priest. Jesus appeared before this body at his trial, and it unjustly condemned him to death." We will again revisit the insecurity of the religious leaders in the next chapter when the resurrected Lazarus is an additional threat to the Jewish leaders' personal empires.

6. Brown, *Death of the Messiah*, 328–97, and concludes that the Sanhedrin had ability to suggest death but was granted by Roman powers.

7. An example of the writer of John using the literary technique known as irony; on the issue of irony in the Gospel of John, see Duke, *Irony in the Fourth Gospel*, 86–87, deal specifically with this pericope.

8. Hence, you see the writer of John introducing his readers to Nicodemus (John 3, 7, 19) and referencing Joseph of Arimathea (John 19:38), two members of the Sanhedrin that saw Jesus was the Messiah. Joseph of Arimathea also appears in the Synoptic Gospels (Matt 27:57; Mark 15:43; Luke 23:50).

Jesus's Special Place

Not only was Jesus about to redeem Israel, he would redeem the whole world.

Raising his good friend from the dead also was the impetus for him withdrawing from Bethany in John 11 near the village of Ephraim (John 11:54).[9] Had there been no threat of danger, Jesus could have remained in Bethany and spent more time with his friends.

Passover Brings Protection

Timing was on Jesus's side and a great Jewish holiday was about to commence. The coming of Passover meant the leaders needed to shift their focus from removing Jesus to being ceremonially clean for the weeklong feast.[10] Jewish people from all over would flock to Jerusalem; hence, the religious leaders could not concentrate on the village of Bethany anymore.[11] There would be too many people around to be able to pull off a murder without being found out. Leaving Bethany earlier after raising Lazarus, due to the threat of Jewish leaders, the canopy of Passover now provided a blanket of protection that will allow Jesus to be reunited with his friends before his passion. Jesus would be safe to travel and on this Friday, he journeys back to Bethany to spend the last days of his role as the Suffering Servant with his disciples and close Bethany friends.

Bethany: Last Place before Resurrection and Last Place before Ascension

There is some evidence that Ephraim would be out of the way for Jesus to return if his final destination was Jerusalem.[12] For Jesus to make the trek back to Bethany showed that there was a higher motive beside convenience.

---

9. The location of this village is uncertain. Lindars, *Gospel of John*, 409–10, lists the three most likely locations of this village and concludes: "Much the best suggestion is that this is the Ephraim mentioned in 2 Samuel 13:23, five miles north-east of Bethel."

10. And could be as long as eight days. It was ironic that the leaders would have to focus on cleansing given their desire to commit murder of an innocent man.

11. But they, the Jewish religious leaders, are very aware of Jesus and aware that the Jews are noticing his absence and want him caught if found in Jerusalem (John 11:55–57).

12. Lindars, *Gospel of John*, 412, writes, "After the questioning of pilgrims in 11:56, we now expect John to bring Jesus to Jerusalem. If Ephraim (11:54) is to be identified with the place near Bethel, he would be coming from the north, and would not need to pass through Bethany."

Before Jesus dies and rises from the dead, he will stay in Bethany, more evidence that Bethany occupies a special place in Jesus's heart. To have an idea of what this pre-resurrection "Bethany stay" was like, Luke gives us a picture of Jesus's first encounter with Bethany in Luke 10:38–42.

Though the name Bethany is not mentioned, Luke refers to a village (Luke 10:38) where Mary and Martha lived (Luke 10:39–42). Since we know Mary and Martha lived in Bethany, it is safe to assume that this is the location of Martha's hospitality meal for Jesus and his disciples.[13] It is Martha who does the inviting and with the invitation comes work. Having to feed Jesus and twelve other men is a huge task, overwhelming for just one. Certainly her sister Mary would understand that there are thirteen guests in their house. They would need food and drink.[14] Mary was oblivious to her sister's toil, having become captivated by Jesus's teaching; she ignored her older sister's need for help and sat at the feet of Jesus. Martha calls to Jesus and implores him to ask her sister to leave his teaching and help serve: "Lord, don't you care that my sister has left me to do the work by myself? Tell her to help me (Luke 10:40)!" Jesus does not give Martha her desired reply but reorients Martha's thinking past the tyranny of the urgent and unto eternity, "Martha, Martha," the Lord answered, "you are worried and upset about many things, but only one thing is needed. Mary has chosen what is better, and it will not be taken away from her" (Luke 10:41–42). Humanity struggles, associating significance with busyness. Somehow, a life where we have little time for others due to vocational, civic, and commercial duties brings acceptance and a good name. Mary and Martha, in Luke 10:38–42, show that Jesus does not value busyness the way humanity does.

The Messiah forges a close friendship with the two sisters, one that is centered on fellowship and discipleship. Though Martha did the inviting, Jesus is the real host and wants the sisters to know that the day-to-day responsibilities of life can blur the priority of eternity and prevent us from sitting at Jesus's feet in a relaxed peaceful fashion. Mary chose better, Jesus was more interested in making the sisters better disciples over being better hosts.

---

13. Meals are a prominent theme in Luke. Barth, *Rediscovering the Lord's Supper*, 71, writes, "In approximately one-fifth of the sentences in Luke's Gospel and in Acts, meals play a conspicuous role." This issue will be more deeply discussed in the next chapter dealing with Saturday.

14. Pao, *Table Fellowship*, 132, writes, "Within the writings of Luke, the relevance of Luke 10:38–42 has also been noted as it is understood to depict the contrast between the ministry of the Word and material care."

Jesus's Special Place

Mary is in direct contrast to the lawyer/law expert in Luke 10:25–37.[15] The law expert seemed more interested in trying to trap Jesus instead of learning from him. Mary does not ask agenda-driven questions like the law expert nor is concerned with the urgent details that adequate hospitality demands, she just sits at Jesus's feet and learns.[16]

Now on this Friday, as Jesus was approaching Bethany, thoughts of their first meal together may have gone through his mind. The next Bethany meal, Martha will make sure all is ready when Jesus arrives, Mary will definitely help to afford her sister the opportunity to sit at the master's feet as she did when he first came to their house.[17] Jesus taught them that to be a growing disciple was more important than being busy; he himself is headed toward a Sabbath rest to cultivate in his soul the replenishment of food, fellowship, friendship, and respite. These meals would be some of Jesus's last before the cross and certainly, knowing he will die eight days from now, Jesus will have much to say.

Meals are more than times of sustenance; he knows there is a banquet to come when the kingdom of God is fully established and this Friday, his last Friday dining as Isaiah's Suffering Servant, will not be his last.[18] The next time he will dine in this fashion will be at the Marriage Supper of the Lamb (Rev 19:9) when the kingdom of God is culminated. These meals together now are just a taste of the future feast that awaits his return. Though no Bethany communication is recorded during Passion Week, one can infer that a lot of teaching was happening after each day's events.

If these scenes were not enough to show Jesus's love for Bethany, Luke 24:50 records that this was the last place on earth Jesus set foot before he ascended to heaven: "When he had led them out to the vicinity of Bethany, he lifted up his hands and blessed them." Jesus loved Bethany so much that it was the last place on earth his feet touched the ground after walking the

---

15. See Green, *Luke*, 434.

16. See Green, *Luke*, 435, where Green argues that this signifies her "status as a disciple (cf. Acts 22:3)." Green goes on to write, "The latter nuance is commended by her activity at his feet: she 'listened to his word.' For the Third Gospel, to listen to the word is to have joined the road of discipleship (e.g., 6:47; 8:11, 21; 11:28)."

17. There is a possibility that the meal could be the Erev Shabbat meal eaten Friday night at the start of Sabbath.

18. Kodell, *Eucharist*, 113, writes, "His meals are harbingers of the banquet to be shared in the kingdom of God. Those who share God's gifts now and hope in his promises must not let complacency rob them of the fulfillment." Meals will be explored more in depth in the next chapter.

earth over thirty-three years.[19] Jesus entered Jerusalem on Palm Sunday from Bethany to accept the mantle of King and would leave this earth in a glorified body from Bethany to return a second time.

But Jesus's final goodbye from Bethany before his second coming is about fifty days away. On the Friday before Good Friday, his feet will touch Bethany without leaving and he will stay there with friends. During the days that follow Jesus will: cleanse the temple physically by moving moneychangers and business people; wither a fig tree, and have another rest day before the Jewish Feast then departing Bethany to have a Passover Meal with his disciples. He will die, rise from the grave, and will say goodbye to these friends forty days after his resurrection in Bethany. With so much significant activity occurring in one locality, clearly Bethany is a place that occupies a special part of Jesus's heart.

---

19. Luke 3:23 reads Jesus was about 30 when he began his ministry. Levites had a training period between ages 25–30 and by age 30, undertook full service (Num 4:47). Jews were also not allowed to read the first few chapters of Ezekiel until they were 30 due to the belief that 30 was a special age of maturity. Most scholars have Jesus being born between 6–4 BC and dying between AD 30–33. Jesus would be between the ages of 34–39 when he died, most likely around 37 years of age, as most place Jesus birth around 5–4 BC and his death in AD 33.

Jesus's Special Place

Questions for Discussion and Personal Reflection

Jesus journeyed from Ephraim to Bethany in John 12:1. It was danger that forced him to leave Bethany (John 11:45–54); is there a place that you would return to despite past danger?

1. Where is your special place? Do you have a special place in your heart like Bethany is to Jesus? How far would you be willing to travel to get there?
2. Where do you have special friends?
3. Where is the most exotic place you have visited?
4. Why do people not always schedule a restful trip? If Jesus made a point to be in Bethany before Good Friday, how does this influence our vacation schedule? Schedule in general?
5. What are some high points in your life that were induced by special places and friends?
6. What were some low places that were induced by places and people who hurt?
7. How often do you travel to these special places and meet special people? How do you avoid the places of hurt?

3

Rest

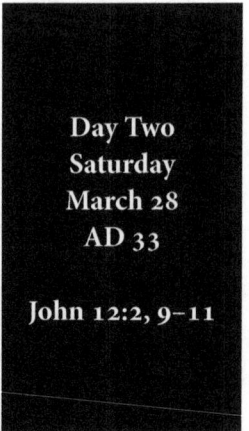

**Day Two
Saturday
March 28
AD 33**

John 12:2, 9–11

Thou hast made us for thyself, O Lord, and our heart is restless until it finds its rest in thee.

—AUGUSTINE OF HIPPO

Let us, therefore, make every effort to enter that rest, so that no one will fall by following their example of disobedience.

—HEBREWS 4:11

THE JOURNEY OF LIFE requires rest from weariness. Whether it is work, school, or any day-to-day matter that depletes the soul, we need rest. Jesus arrived in Bethany before sundown Friday and spent the Sabbath with his friends. It is now Saturday; Jesus would be finishing the Sabbath and will engage in the evening meal.[1] It was highly unlikely that Jesus spent his Sabbath sleeping all day or being idle. John does not record Jesus's activities but we can infer that he went to a nearby synagogue to teach from the Scriptures (Luke 4:16–20, 31–32; 6:6; 13:10, 18–21), or exorcised a demon, or healed someone who was sick (Luke 4:33–39; 6:7–11; 13:11–17). Doing miracles on the Sabbath was nothing new; the New Testament records Jesus performing seven. Luke records five (Luke 4:33–38; 6:6–11; 13:10–17; 14:1–4) while John records two more Sabbath healings (John 5:1–15; 9:1–34), but even if Jesus did these things, he would have rested.

What else did Jesus do on the Sabbath? He probably had a simple meal in the afternoon, like the one with a Pharisee in Luke 14:1–24.[2] The food

---

1. See Beasley-Murray, *John*, 208; Brown, *Gospel according to John*, 447, writes, "We must presume that the Sabbath had come to an end, or Martha could not be serving at table." As discussed earlier, there are some discrepancies between John 12:1 and John 12:2. Scholars are divided on whether or not 12:1–2 are one day or in the case here, John 12:1 is Friday and John 12:2 and 9–11 are Saturday.

2. See Green, *Luke*, 545–50, for more details into the specific meal Jesus had with the Pharisees who would be part of the social elite of the day.

would have been prepared the day before. Jesus may have also spent the time in prayer, teaching, discipling, and studying Scripture.[3] The writer of John does not give the details but we can infer from the evidence found in other gospels. Regardless of what Jesus did, he tried to rest, and would be ready to face the most important week of his life. Human history will be in his hands. The world would never be the same.

Jesus valued rest and scheduled it. In Mark 6:31, the writer states that Jesus specifically tells his disciples to "come away by yourselves to a desolate place and rest a while." Jesus recognized that life is taxing and proactively initiates rest for his disciples. This rest in Mark 6:31 was beyond the Sabbath, but a rest brought on by an inordinately busy schedule and tiring circumstances, much as humanity endures today.[4] It is not uncommon for the writer of Mark to record Jesus taking his disciples away for seasons of respite and teaching. R. T. France writes, "Such 'retreats' are sometimes in the hills (3:13–19; 9:2; cf. 6:46), but any place which is away from other people . . . will serve."[5] The need to withdraw from people was due to Jesus's wide popularity; crowds of people would gather around him for teaching and healing. This meant hard labor for Jesus and his disciples; hence, the need to draw back. So often, the best thing to do in our own lives is not to work more, but to withdraw, rest, recharge so we can be more effective when work is reengaged.

The writer of Mark highlights Jesus's "alone times" away from teaching, preaching and ministering to physical and spiritual infirmities. During this alone time with the disciples, Jesus instructed, explaining to his disciples the meaning of parables (Mark 4:10, 34). He took three disciples to witness the transfiguration (Mark 9:2–8). He took disciples from work to answer questions and explain what they did wrong (Mark 9:28–29).[6]

---

3. In light of Matt 9:14–17; Mark 2:18–22; Luke 5:33–39, it is unlikely that Jesus would have been fasting given his discourse on why he and his disciples do not fast since Jesus has inaugurated the kingdom which is a feast as described in Rev 19:9. Weddings in all cultures are festive occasions filled with feasting. A Jewish celebration would last a week. In the OT, fasting was often associated with remorse or sadness.

4. Though it was Jesus's desire to have a period of rest, the crowds did not comply, reaching Jesus's destination before he does (Mark 6:33). Jesus had compassion on the people and thus ensues the feeding of the 5,000 (which would be many more because this number does not include women and children).

5. France, *Gospel of Mark*, 263–64.

6. Ibid.

Jesus himself cultivated the discipline of spending time alone for prayer before work (Mark 1:35–39).[7] He knew he needed it due to the great amount of labor he faced. No longer could he enter into a town openly but needed to stay outside in lonely places (Mark 1:45).[8] Jesus had so much work that it made him extremely tired; a deep storm could not wake him from sleep (Mark 4:35–41). Rest was valued.

Many of us use a busy, tiring schedule as a "red badge of significance," importance can be tied to exhaustion and an overtaxing schedule. Dr. Brené Brown writes in *The Gifts of Imperfection*, "If we want to live a wholehearted life, we have to become intentional about cultivating rest and play, and we must work to let go of exhaustion as a status symbol and productivity as self-worth."[9] Jewish theologian Rabbi Abraham Heschel writes:

> The meaning of the Sabbath is to celebrate time rather than space. Six days a week we live under the tyranny of things of space; on the Sabbath we try to become attuned to holiness in time. It is a day on which we are called upon to share in what is eternal in time, to turn from the results of creation to the mystery of creation, from the world of creation to the creation of the world.[10]

We see on this Saturday that the writer of John did not give any details about Jesus's activities, though we can infer that he was not idle; we can also infer that he engaged in rest.

Humanity values accomplishment as a buoy of significance; if a calendar or day planner is presented where busyness is not present, shame can ensue. Thoughts of unworthiness, judgment, and unlovability can arise. People idolize a heavy work calendar or overburdened logbooks as emblems of meaning. Rest is rarely a topic of personal pride. A "badge of shame" can be attached to someone who is not busy or sleep deprived.[11]

---

7. France, *Gospel of Mark*, 111–14.

8. France writes, "Thus in a few quick strokes Mark has painted a powerful picture of Jesus's 'success' and of the problems it is already beginning to cause. It will be important to bear this popular response to Jesus in mind as the opposition develops in succeeding scenes; his opponents do not represent the majority opinion" (ibid., 121).

9. Brown, *Gifts of Imperfection*, 102; see also Brown, *Daring Greatly*.

10. Heschel, *Sabbath*, 10.

11. Harvard Medical School lists six reason why sleep is so important (http://www.health.harvard.edu/press_releases/importance_of_sleep_and_health):

> 1. Learning and memory: Sleep helps the brain commit new information to memory through a process called memory consolidation. In studies, people who'd slept after learning a task did better on tests later.

Though Jesus had an inordinately busy schedule, he always made time to draw back for prayer, time with God (Luke 5:12–16), and rest (Mark 6:31). People view rest as an enemy of productivity and accomplishment but nine days before Easter, Jesus prepares for the most important week of humanity by resting. Rest was scheduled and should be added to our datebooks and diaries.

On Saturday, he is finishing his rest and about to eat a meal with the disciples and Bethany friends. One week from today, his body would rest in a tomb owned by Joseph of Arimathea while his spirit was in heaven before the Father (Heb 8:1—10:18). Before the most important week of Jesus's life where he would fulfill his mission and finish paying for humanities' sins, he took time to rest. If we are feeling burned out, tired, and careworn, we should schedule rest like Jesus did.

---

2. Metabolism and weight: Chronic sleep deprivation may cause weight gain by affecting the way our bodies process and store carbohydrates, and by altering levels of hormones that affect our appetite.

3. Safety: Sleep debt contributes to a greater tendency to fall asleep during the daytime. These lapses may cause falls and mistakes such as medical errors, air traffic mishaps, and road accidents.

4. Mood: Sleep loss may result in irritability, impatience, inability to concentrate, and moodiness. Too little sleep can also leave you too tired to do the things you like to do.

5. Cardiovascular health: Serious sleep disorders have been linked to hypertension, increased stress hormone levels, and irregular heartbeat.

6. Disease: Sleep deprivation alters immune function, including the activity of the body's killer cells. Keeping up with sleep may also help fight cancer.

Questions for Discussion and Personal Reflection

Are you tired and weary? Is there anything you can do to refresh yourself?

1. Do you observe a Sabbath? Why or why not?
2. How can we make our Sabbaths more restful?
3. What are some ways you schedule in rest and play?
4. Have you ever had trouble sleeping? What did you do to overcome this?
5. Are vacations more stressful than work? If so, why? How could you improve the quality of your vacations?
6. How do you rest spiritually? Does meditation help? What are verses that we can meditate on more?
7. Are there people in your life who refresh you? Who? How can you spend regular time with them?
8. Are there people in your life that drain you? How can you form a boundary to prevent them from exhausting you more?

4

Martha's Metamorphosis

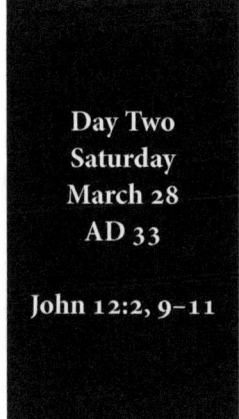

Day Two
Saturday
March 28
AD 33

John 12:2, 9–11

Worship is our response to the overtures of love from the heart of the Father.

—RICHARD FOSTER

"Martha, Martha," the Lord answered, "you are worried and upset about many things, but only one thing is needed Mary has chosen what is better."

—LUKE 10:41–42

IT IS NOT A surprise that Martha is described in John 12:2 serving the meal. She was once a very restless soul but we can now infer that she has learned to sit at Jesus's feet like her sister Mary. No longer does the gospel writer point to her emphasis on action, no longer will the gospel writer highlight her pragmatism (Luke 10:38–42; John 11:21, 39). Martha has transformed from doer to worshipper.

John 12:2 was the last time Martha's name appears in the New Testament; the first time she is mentioned is found in Luke 10:38–42. Before this final mention, her name is synonymous with action over faith. From Luke's text, the first meeting between Jesus and Martha introduced us to her struggle (Luke 10:38).[1] Clearly Martha's personality was one of works, a person who valued productivity. She is a classic "doer"; hence, Jesus contrasted her actions with her sister's to illustrate the importance of discipleship and the need to be still, listen, and learn. Mary sitting at the feet of Jesus is a form of surrender and worship to Christ's lordship while Martha's activities are distracting her from a chance to hear and worship the Savior.

Doers like Martha often seek their self-worth and sense of acceptance from the praises and recognition of people; a task needs to be performed

---

1. The writer of Luke describing Martha in Luke 10:38 as "a woman named Martha welcomed him into her house" sounds like a first meeting rather than a previous relationship. Contrast to John 11:5 when the writer describes her as "loved" by Jesus.

well. In Luke 10:40 alone, Martha uses the personal pronouns of "my" and "me" three times. At the heart of being a doer is a need for success, even perfectionism, as the motivation.

The Bible definitely encourages living life well; the Apostle Paul always exhorts his disciples to walk in a manner worthy of the Lord (1 Thess 2:12; Col 1:10; Eph 4:1; Phil 3:17–18), but this walk is fueled by worship of God, not by earning it through good works (Eph 2:8–10). Martha, like many of us, may have faced this struggle early on.

Fast Friends

There is clearly a special connection between Jesus and Martha (Luke 10:38–42). Just as David quickly connected with Jonathan on a spiritual level (1 Sam 18:1), a similar connection occurs between Jesus and his beloved Bethany friends. When Martha's name next appears, she, along with her siblings, is referred to as loved by Jesus (John 11:1, 5, 36). Of course Jesus loves everyone, but the writer of John is clearly drawing a distinction, highlighting a special bond Jesus has with Martha, Mary, and Lazarus. From Luke to John, as we have seen in previous chapters, it is clear that the Bethany beloved held a special place in Jesus's heart.

Relationships are an art, not a science. There are some people who have been afforded countless hours, days, and even years of emotional expenditure yet never progress beyond a shallow, uncomfortable level. There are also individuals we first meet with whom a deeper level of connection develops within five minutes than with some people whom we have known for years. Jesus clearly had a special connection with Martha and her siblings.

John's Portrayal: Doer to Worshipper

John's portrayal of Martha is very similar to Luke's, a woman of action. After her brother dies, she goes out to meet Jesus while Mary remains in the home (John 11:20). Martha rebukes Jesus by telling him he was too late; had he arrived sooner, Lazarus could have lived. Jesus is about to take Martha to the next level of her faith journey (John 11:21). It is clear Martha did not believe Jesus could resurrect her brother; when Jesus orders Lazarus's tomb to be opened, she brazenly says that the tomb would stink due to her brother being dead for four days (John 11:39). She is about to have her world rocked and would not have to wait for heaven to see her brother again.

Lazarus is raised (John 11:40–44). After the miracle, we hear nothing in the Bible of Martha's future belief, but clearly she has taken a step in her journey. As Martha is serving Jesus the meal this Saturday evening, these thoughts are probably fresh in her mind.

The dinner is about to begin, commemorating the ending of Sabbath; Martha is serving it in Jesus's honor. Now Martha knows that her dear friend has power beyond her comprehension.[2] Her mourning has turned to joy but in less than a week, she will mourn again as her dear friend, the Savior and Messiah, will suffer on a cross and become a curse for humankind (Gal 3:13). Martha will remember her Lord raising Lazarus and will likely remember her Lord's words of himself rising again. She will cry and mourn but there will be a part of her heart that knows Messiah's tomb will not be stinky. She thought her brother's tomb would have a stench after four days, but after three days, her dear friend will rise and Martha will be ready for another meal.[3]

It is a time of rest where one has the time to slow down stop and be able to reflect on God's goodness in life. Martha has had time to reflect on hers, how she valued doing over worshipping; how she knew Jesus could heal her brother when Lazarus was alive and sick, and how she doubted after Lazarus had been dead for four days. The Sabbath has ended and Martha served Jesus, remembering how he miraculously raised her brother. This Saturday evening meal will prepare her for Jesus's death, but in nine days, Jesus will be the one who rises, further growing Martha's faith and helping her live a life of worship over action.

---

2. We will discuss Mary's anointing of Jesus later as well as reference the anointing in an appendix.

3. Though no other meal in Bethany is recorded, Jesus went back to heaven from Bethany so we can infer that the forty days after the resurrection could have included more time in Bethany.

Questions for Discussion and Personal Reflection

Why is it so easy to overlook worship for work as Martha did?

1. Have you ever been or are you currently in a hopeless situation like Martha was in: her brother being dead for 4 days left no hope for resuscitation? How can Jesus's resurrection power offer us hope in our current challenging circumstances?
2. How did Martha's faith grow when she realized that Jesus was indeed the Son of God with the power to resurrect the dead?
3. Are reflection and meditation over God's goodness and workings in your life regular components in your spiritual journey?
4. How would life change if the day were begun in prayer, Scripture reading and meditation instead of the hustle and hurry of life? What needs to happen to lessen the hustle and increase the reflection?
5. What great acts has God done for you to cause you to grow in your faith journey?

5

Meals

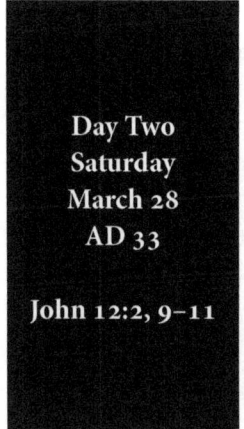

**Day Two
Saturday
March 28
AD 33**

John 12:2, 9–11

One cannot think well, love well, sleep well, if one has not dined well.

—VIRGINIA WOOLF

Jesus said to them, "Come and have breakfast."

—JOHN 21:12

FOOD ENHANCES LIFE'S JOURNEY; Jesus clearly enjoyed it. John 12:2 portrayed a meal in his honor.[1] It would be highly unlikely that this meal would be in the afternoon, Sabbath would still be observed and all preparations would have been completed the day before, not the milieu for an honorary feast. Most likely Mary, Martha, and possibly others began preparing for this meal at the very latest at Saturday's sunset. To have a meal in someone's honor probably communicates a more elaborate banquet than what would appear on a Sabbath afternoon. The writer of John was setting the stage for another meal scene in ch. 13 where Jesus would serve his disciples by washing their feet, but this meal would not occur for another six days; on this Saturday evening after Sabbath has concluded, Jesus was the one to be served.[2]

This Saturday evening meal may have been a thank offering the Bethany sisters wanted to give Jesus for reviving their brother from the dead. Because of the threat of the Jewish religious leaders after the miraculous raising of Lazarus, Jesus had to withdraw to a safer place, Ephraim. The sisters probably wanted to do something for Jesus soon after their brother's resurrection but he could not stay in Bethany. Before the Savior would

---

1. The Greek word used here, according to Morris, *Gospel according to John*, 575, "appears to mean the main meal of the day, held towards evening."

2. There is an issue with the chronology of the anointing of Jesus in John with the record of the Synoptics. See section discussing the anointing of Jesus in John 12:3–8 titled "A Bracketed Bethany Anointing" for discussion on John's chronology vs. the Synoptics.

suffer for humanity's sins, he returned to the village to rest and partake of a special meal in his honor.

Though there are no details of the Saturday evening meal, we can infer that Jesus taught (cf. Luke 10:38–42). Martha was probably more prepared for the meal this time, not stressed out to get food on the table, and was able to sit at Jesus's feet with her brother, Lazarus, and sister, Mary. Most likely, Jesus was informing the Bethany beloved that he would die during the Passover holiday. Prior to Passion Week, Jesus spoke of his death multiple times (Mark 8:31; 9:31; 10:33–34), and each time told his disciples he would rise from the dead, but his disciples did not understand what he was saying. Mary did and four days later will anoint her master with a highly valuable perfume. In seven days, Jesus will perish and his disciples will scatter, but Mary and her siblings will have a much different perspective. They know they will see their master again. But tonight, everyone will eat.

Biblical Significance of Meals

Meals played a significant role in Jesus's time on earth. In six days, Jesus would preside over the Passover feast and teach his disciples that his death will fulfill all the ancient prophecies while enacting a new covenant (Matt 26:17–30; Mark 14:12–25; Luke 22:17–20; 1 Cor 11:23–25). This would be the last time he ate with them before his death but more meals would follow his resurrection (Luke 24; John 21). After he rose from the dead, he appeared to his disciples at least three more times (John 20:19–23, 24–29; 21:1–25). In the evening of Easter, Jesus appeared to his disciples and ate (Luke 24:36–49; John 20:19–23). On his third biblical appearance, he had breakfast of fish and bread with them on a beach. Meals are an integral part of Jesus's life and ministry; it is not a surprise that one of the last recorded appearances Jesus had with his followers occurred over a meal (John 21:1–14). However, on this Saturday evening, Jesus partook in a feast given by his Bethany beloved. It is a celebratory meal, the last one before Jesus died but definitely not the last time they would feast together. Jesus will feast again with them at the Marriage Supper of the Lamb (Rev 19:9).

For all, food is part of life. Some may see food as a means of subsistence, but for the biblical culture, meals possess a spiritual and communal meaning. With so much time spent on the repast, it is no surprise that Jesus used meals as a way to communicate the gospel message to unbelievers and as a method of discipleship in teaching his followers. Much of Jesus's ministry occurred over meals.

Luke and Secular Meals

None of the other three gospels matches Luke's eating records. With so much time spent dining, it is not a surprise that the writer of Luke records many of Jesus's meals, 19 total and 13 that are specific to Luke.[3] Jesus used the mealtime as a significant aspect of fulfilling his purpose on earth. Robert Karris writes, "There is considerable truth in what one wag said about Luke's Gospel: Jesus is either going to a meal, at a meal, or coming from a meal."[4] It is obvious that the mealtime is a significant time Jesus used in his ministry.

Eating together is more than just filling up on food; in biblical times, it represents an association and acceptance of the individual(s) one is dining with. Dennis E. Smith writes:

> Table fellowship is a symbol of community fellowship. The table designates a special relationship between those who sit at the same table. Jesus eats with sinners and tax collectors (Luke 5:27–32; 7:34; 15:2). He goes to the house of Zacchaeus (Luke 19:1–9). The table is for the oppressed, handicapped and disenfranchised (Luke 7:22; 14:12–14).[5]

Meals carry a deeper biblical meaning than just sustenance and consumption; the Scriptures communicate a social, spiritual, and communal dimension.

Secular studies also affirm that meals have a deeper meaning to various groups and cultures. For one, meals have shown to be markers of a nation's history.[6] Food choices driven by culture and forms of consumption

---

3. Powell, *Introducing the New Testament*, 158. See also Neyrey, *Ceremonies in Luke-Acts*, 361–87; Kelley, *Meals with Jesus*, 613–38.

4. Karris, *Luke*, 47.

5. Smith, *Table Fellowship*, 614. Also Jeremias, *Proclamation of Jesus*, 115, writes: In Judaism . . . table-fellowship means fellowship before God, for the eating of a piece of broken bread by everyone who shares in the meal brings out the fact that they all have a share in the blessing which the master of the house had spoken over the unbroken bread. Thus, Jesus's meals with the publicans and sinners . . . are not only events on a social level but had an even deeper significance. . . . The inclusion of sinners into the community of salvation, achieved in table-fellowship, is the most meaningful expression of the message of the redeeming love of God.

6. Bell and Valentine, *Consuming*, 168, write, "The history of any nation's diet is the

ultimately came to be grasped as "distinguishing" of citizens and nation.[7] Meals are also a marker for a people group's cultural identity.[8] Just as there is biblical evidence arguing that food and the sharing of it communicate an association and acceptance, secular studies have shown that this thought still persists today. Food is a mode of communication that "articulates notions of inclusion and exclusion, of national pride and xenophobia."[9] In both secular studies as well as biblical, to dine with someone is to share in an aspect of one's essence as well as communicate acceptance. Repast consumption is a significant aspect of being.[10]

Jesus has dined with the socially elite (Luke 14:1–6ff.) as well the socially rejected (Luke 5:27–39). For our Lord, the gospel message is for all and he communicates humanity's equality in dining with everyone. But this Saturday evening meal is different; fellowship will be paramount. Mary and Martha want to communicate nobility and gratitude toward Jesus. He is staying with them and is now the guest of honor at an end of the Sabbath celebratory meal.

---

history of the nation itself, with food, fashion, fads and fancies mapping episodes of colonialism and migration, trade and exploration, cultural exchange and boundary-marking."

7. So is the premise of Tannahill, *Food in History*.

8. Kittler and Sucher, *Food and Culture*, 5, write, "Eating, like dressing in traditional clothing or speaking in a native language, is a daily reaffirmation of cultural identity." See also Strauss, *The Raw and the Cooked*, as the argument is that food is a philological that imitates the assembly and body of society. Palmer, "From Theory to Practice," 194, writes, "Rituals and practices relating to food consumption are often used to define and maintain boundaries of identity; boundaries that serve to define the identity of a minority ethnic community from the dominant core identity of the nation with which it resides." Her thoughts have been a good guide to the secular aspect of meals as deeper than just consumption for sustenance.

9. Bell and Valentine, *Consuming*, 168.

10. See also Stein, *Luke*, 182.

Questions for Discussion and Personal Reflection

Why do so many intimate interactions occur over a meal? Why do you think the mealtime is so special?

1. Studies also show that children who have regular meals as a family do better; if true, why do you think this is the case?
2. How much time do you spend preparing and consuming meals?
3. How can the church today use meals more like Jesus did?
4. How can we personally use meals to enhance our ministry? Life?

6

Dealing with Toxic People

I think anybody with an insecurity, which is everyone, appreciates the fact that it's much easier to be a predator than it is to be the prey.

—JAMES VAN DER BEEK

Then the Pharisees went out and began to plot with the Herodians how they might kill Jesus.

—MARK 3:6

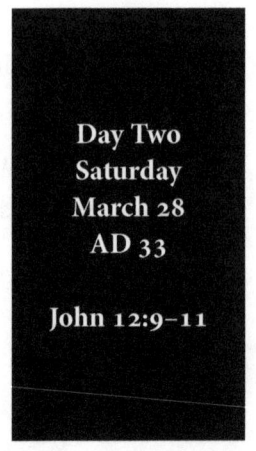

Day Two
Saturday
March 28
AD 33

John 12:9–11

LIFE'S JOURNEY WILL ENCOUNTER toxic people. The Bible refers to them as "enemies." An enemy is "a person who feels hatred for, fosters harmful designs against, or engages in antagonistic activities against another."[1]

There are continuums. Aggressors aspire to varying degrees of atrocity; but regardless of where they are, all seek pleasure in pain.[2] Jesus encountered many who wanted to do him harm. Even while he was partaking in the Saturday evening meal, people were plotting against him (John 12:10–11). As we will see here and in following chapters, throughout the next nine days, toxic people occupy much of Jesus's time.

One would think the Roman government would feel the most threatened by the Messiah. Certainly the Roman leaders were familiar with King David of Israel and how he led the nation to many magnificent military victories. Surely the Roman government would know that the Jewish people believed the Messiah would be the next King David, a threat to Roman

---

1. Dictionary.com, s.v. "enemy."
2. In biblical studies, there is an academic reference to the German word *Schadenfreude*, with the literal meaning of taking delight in the suffering of others. See Gilmour, "Delighting in the Sufferings of Others, 129–39.

safety in a time of great peace.³ One of the main Roman phrases was "peace and security."⁴

Over thirty years ago, Herod, the appointed king of Judea by Rome, felt threatened when the magi came to Jerusalem to worship Jesus (Matt 2:1–12). But the threat seemed to have died with Herod in 4 BC. Rome easily could have tracked Jesus down but did not.

The threat came from a completely unlikely source: Jewish religious leaders. They knew Scriptures thoroughly and had evidence that events foretold in Isa 29:18–19 and 35:5–6 were happening. Worship should have flowed from the religious leaders' hearts as it did from the magi, who saw evidence that a king would be born and traveled a great distance to worship him. However, the leaders could not see Jesus as the Davidic King who would rule forever.⁵

Not only could they not see that Jesus was the Messiah, but they could not accept that Jesus had raised Lazarus from the dead. Blinded by their wealth, power, and position, the Jewish religious leaders saw the Lord as a menace to their personal empires. While many were bowing down and worshipping Jesus, the leaders wanted to kill both the Messiah and Lazarus to preserve their personal domains (John 12:3–11). When people feel threatened, fear blinds! Elimination of the threat is pursued instead of self-examination and repentance. Rather than dealing with their personal issues, removing the object of anxiety became the chosen irrational pathway.

Pride, a progeny of shame, blinded the normally pious and righteous Jewish religious leaders. They plotted to break one of the Ten

---

3. See Tite, *Pax, Peace and the New Testament*, 301–24:
The Jewish, Greek, Roman and Christian perceptions of peace were not wholly different—though clearly not wholly the same. A transcultural approach to the Mediterranean region (a Pan-Mediterranean milieu) explained the correspondence of these cultural groups. An interactive dynamic existed in the first century, which drew the various cultural components of the Roman Empire together. As a result of this study, the antithetical relationship that scholarship has drawn between the Christian peace and the Pax Romana cannot be held. Rather, a close cultural connection must be seen between the Christian peace and the Roman peace. (324)

4. For close to two hundred years during the first and second centuries AD, there was very little military activity and wars, an ideal environment for Jesus to be born into given that the history of the region has been one of conflict.

5. The first record of Jesus's conflict with the religious leaders is in Mark 2:1–12 when he heals the paralytic on the mat. Jesus's pronouncement of the paralytic's sins being forgiven is a claim to deity. Many scholars acknowledge that even the Jewish Messiah is not deity. Hence, Jesus's early claims was not Davidic but to deity which alarmed the leaders.

Commandments—thou shalt not kill—not once, but twice. In order to accomplish this dual murder, they would need to break another commandment of the Decalogue: thou shall not bear false witness.

Toxic people in this world always surround us, and they can come from the least likely of places. Despite God's mighty work in raising Lazarus, the miracle elicited fear and threats, not worship, from many Jewish religious leaders who possessed a deep knowledge of the Torah, but had forgotten its meaning.

The religious leaders were even more anxious as a result of this Saturday evening meal. After Lazarus was raised from the dead, the leaders ordered the Jewish people to report the Messiah's whereabouts (John 11:57). The motive for seeking this information was clear: capture. In John 12:9, the reader is alerted to a "large crowd of Jews"[6] who discovered Jesus's location; however, rather than obey the religious leaders' directive, they chose not to disclose Jesus's location.[7]

The leaders' worst fears became reality: Jesus's following was growing. John wrote in 12:11 "many of the Jews were going over to Jesus and putting their faith in him." The leaders' fears were expressed in John 11:48: "If we let him go on like this, everyone will believe in him, and then the Romans will come and take away both our temple and our nation." These fears were coming to fruition in 12:9–11 as the crowds of Jews are not recorded as obeying the decree of the Sanhedrin, but putting their faith in Jesus. Though he would die in a week, the Jewish leaders' fears are fulfilled forty years later, in AD 70, when Rome indeed destroyed the temple, took away the nation, and scattered the Jews[8] across the empire. Israel would not be a nation again until 1948.

Jesus knew he would die for humanity. Despite evil leaders who had presented danger throughout his all too brief ministry, Jesus enjoyed this Saturday evening meal commemorating the end of Sabbath with his disciples and Bethany friends who worshipped him as Lord.

---

6. Michaels, *Gospel of John*, 673n54, states that other scholars (Bultmann and Raymond Brown) identify the crowd with John 11:42.

7. See ibid., 673–74.

8. This is often referred to as the Diaspora.

Biblical Portrayal of Toxic People

The Bible has illustrated from cover to cover how sin makes people toxic. Jesus knew this and did not entrust himself to individuals very easily (John 2:24–25). Perhaps this is one reason Jesus was so drawn to his beloved friends in Bethany—Mary, Martha, and Lazarus—he trusted them.

In Genesis 3 and 4, the toxicity of sin is apparent. Sin entered the world through Adam and Eve's disobedience and continued with Cain's murder of his brother Abel. God had confronted Cain before his sin and warned him in Gen 4:7: "If you do well, will you not be accepted? And if you do not do well, sin is crouching at the door. Its desire is for you, but you must rule over it." But Cain failed. Why did Jesus not entrust himself to many? He knew sin was crouching at humanity's door, and many could not master it. Cain eventually killed his brother, unable to rule over sin, rather than dealing with his own issues of unacceptability. Instead of trying to do better, he chose to eliminate the object of his insecurity and commit murder, much like the Jewish religious leaders would do to Jesus in seven days.

The whole of Scripture shows how utterly depraved human nature is and how utterly loving God is to redeem this depraved creation back to himself. In the New Jerusalem, people will no longer be toxic because sin will be demolished. But until that day, humanity must press on, trying not to allow sin to have mastery.

Criticism: Marker for Doing God's Will

If one is doing the will and works of God, criticism will come. Jesus's life was filled with unwarranted criticism because he was doing the will of the Father (see Mark 2:6–7, 24; 3:6, 22; 7:1–5). It is vital that a Christ-follower focus on pleasing God. Humanity is fickle and will disappoint us if we give our heart away.

Paul dealt with criticism by focusing on Jesus (see 1 Cor 2:2; 4:1–5; Col 3:1–4). Toxic people exist because all have sinned and fall short of the glory of God. These people want to do us harm emotionally, verbally, physically, economically, and spiritually. How did Jesus specifically deal with the Pharisees, Sadducees, Herodians, teachers of the law, scribes, and Sanhedrin, who all wanted him dead? Before we explore how Jesus dealt with toxic people, we will consider what they look like.

Characteristics of Toxic People

Like Jesus, we will encounter toxic people in our lives. The following is a list of ten types of toxic people of which many encompass the religious leaders:[9]

1. The Gossip

"Great minds discuss ideas, average ones discuss events, and small minds discuss people" (Eleanor Roosevelt).

Gossipers derive pleasure from other people's misfortunes. It might be fun to peer into somebody else's personal or professional faux pas at first, but over time, it gets tiring, makes you feel gross, and hurts other people. There are too many positives out there and too much to learn from interesting people to waste your time talking about the misfortune of others.

2. The Temperamental

Some people have absolutely no control over their emotions. They will lash out at you and project their feelings onto you, all the while thinking that you're the one causing their malaise. Temperamental people are tough to dump from your life because their lack of control over their emotions makes you feel bad for them. When push comes to shove though, temperamental people will use you as their emotional toilet and should be avoided at all costs.

3. The Victim

Victims are tough to identify because you initially empathize with their problems. But as time passes, you begin to realize that their "time of need" is *all the time*. Victims actively push away any personal responsibility by making every speed bump they encounter into an uncrossable mountain. They don't see tough times as opportunities to learn and grow from; instead, they see them as an out. There's an old saying: "Pain is inevitable but suffering is optional." It perfectly captures the toxicity of the victim, who chooses to suffer every time.

---

9. The following list was taken from Dr. Travis Bradberry, "10 Toxic People You Should Avoid at All Costs," *LinkedIn*, August 30, 2015 (https://www.linkedin.com/pulse/toxic-people-you-should-avoid-all-costs-dr-travis-bradberry). See also Deborah Ward, "Top 10 Traits of Unsafe People," *Psychology Today* website, November 16, 2013 (https://www.psychologytoday.com/blog/sense-and-sensitivity/201311/the-top-10-traits-unsafe-people) for a list of toxic people traits where unsafe was used in the article but I have changed unsafe to toxic.

4. The Self-Absorbed

Self-absorbed people bring you down through the impassionate distance they maintain from other people. You can usually tell when you're hanging around self-absorbed people because you start to feel completely alone. This happens because as far as they're concerned, there's no point in having a real connection between them and anyone else. You're merely a tool used to build their self-esteem.

5. The Envious

To envious people, the grass is always greener somewhere else. Even when something great happens to envious people, they don't derive any satisfaction from it. This is because they measure their fortune against the world's when they should be deriving their satisfaction from within. And let's face it, there's *always* someone out there who's doing better if you look hard enough. Spending too much time around envious people is dangerous because they teach you to trivialize your own accomplishments.

6. The Manipulator

Manipulators suck time and energy out of your life under the façade of friendship. They can be tricky to deal with because they treat you like a friend. They know what you like, what makes you happy, and what you think is funny, but the difference is that they use this information as part of a hidden agenda. Manipulators always want something from you, and if you look back on your relationships with them, it's all take, take, take, with little or no giving. They'll do anything to win you over just so they can work you over.

7. The Dementor

In J. K. Rowling's *Harry Potter* series, Dementors are evil creatures that suck people's souls out of their bodies, leaving them merely as shells of humans. Whenever a Dementor enters the room, it goes dark, people get cold, and they begin to recall their worst memories. Rowling said that she developed the concept for Dementors based on highly negative people—the kind of people who have the ability to walk into a room and instantly suck the life out of it.

Dementors suck the life out of the room by imposing their negativity and pessimism upon everyone they encounter. Their viewpoints are always glass half empty, and they can inject fear and concern into even the most benign situations. A Notre Dame University study found that students assigned to roommates who thought negatively were far more likely to develop negative thinking and even depression themselves.

8. The Twisted

There are certain toxic people who have bad intentions, deriving deep satisfaction from the pain and misery of others. They are either out to hurt you, to make you feel bad, or to get something from you; otherwise, they have no interest in you. The only good thing about this type is that you can spot their intentions quickly, which makes it that much faster to get them out of your life.

9. The Judgmental

Judgmental people are quick to tell you exactly what is and isn't cool. They have a way of taking the thing you're most passionate about and making you feel terrible about it. Instead of appreciating and learning from people who are different from them, judgmental people look down on others. Judgmental people stifle your desire to be a passionate, expressive person, so you're best off cutting them out and being yourself.

10. The Arrogant

Arrogant people are a waste of your time because they see everything you do as a personal challenge. Arrogance is false confidence, and it always masks major insecurities. A University of Akron study found that arrogance is correlated with a slew of problems in the workplace. Arrogant people tend to be lower performers, more disagreeable, and have more cognitive problems than the average person.

Jesus's Response to the Religious Leaders

We know that people are toxic by nature because of sin. We also know that Jesus did not entrust himself to humanity very easily. Because Jesus was doing the will of God, he experienced abundant criticism, especially from the Jewish religious leaders. How did he deal with them?[10] The following are different excerpts from the Gospels on how Jesus dealt with toxic people.

1. *Know When You Need to Withdraw*[11]

---

10. The following points are aided by the material from psychologist Dr. William Gaultiere of *Soul Shepherding* (http://www.soulshepherding.org/2012/07/jesus-way-of-dealing-with-anger) and has been used via permission from him and edited for the purposes of this section. Any footnotes are mine.

11. The Greek verb translated "withdraw" is often used in the context of danger.

The religious leaders plotted to kill Jesus after he healed a man with a shriveled hand on the Sabbath, so *he withdrew* (Matt 12:9–14).[12]

In Matt 16:1–4, religious leaders tried pressuring Jesus to show them a sign from heaven to prove himself. He told them they were missing the signs right in front of them, acknowledging that their request was evil. The only sign they would receive was that of Jonah.[13] *He walked away.*

From John 10:22–42: They picked up stones to stone Jesus when he proclaimed, "I and the Father are one." He confronted them for wanting to stone him even after he had done so many wonderful miracles. When they came after him, *he escaped.*

Do not engage a toxic person for too long. Move away from such persons as quickly as you can. Proverbs 26:4 states not to engage fools according to their folly. Jesus, rather than trying to win, does not engage too long and withdraws. When engaged in difficult circumstances, especially when we own personal innocence, we often seek to vindicate ourselves; but trying to be vindicated by those who are toxic only fuels the fire of insecurity. Walking away is the most victorious acquittal.

2. *Remain Calm*

The leaders accused Jesus of being in league with Satan after he delivered a possessed man. Jesus *calmly explained* that there was a war between the kingdom of God and the kingdom of Satan (Matt 12:22–37).

Engaging with toxic people can be emotional. Rationality becomes endangered. Remaining calm is paramount or the situation can escalate.

3. *Ask a Question*

The leaders criticized Jesus and his disciples for picking heads of grain on the Sabbath. *Jesus asked them* if they had read the Scriptures instructing that the Sabbath is about God's mercy, not sacrifice (Matt 12:1–8).

This changes the attitude of the debate. When we respond with defensive statements, toxic people go on the offensive; but questions can defuse attacks and change the tone.

4. *Sometimes Answer a Question with a Question*

---

12. Religious leaders encompass: Pharisee, Sadducees, Herodians, and teachers of the law, scribes, and the Sanhedrin. Luke 19:47 also refers to "first ones" among the people, usually translated as leaders or principal men who could be religious leaders or just lay leaders.

13. Note the pairing of the Pharisees with the Sadducees, a phenomenon unique to Matthew. Despite their extreme ideological and theological differences, they unite against Jesus.

The religious leaders challenged Jesus by asking, "By what authority are you doing these things?" Before Jesus would respond, he insisted they *answer his question* about whether John's baptism came from heaven or men. The religious leaders ultimately refused to answer because they realized they had been caught in their own trap. If they said John was from men, then the people would be mad at them; but if they admitted that God sent John, then they were admitting that God sent Jesus, too. Since the religious leaders did not answer his question, Jesus did not respond to their enquiry either (Matt 21:23-27).

Many times, toxic people do not ask a question because they want your answer. Instead, they are using their question as a personal attack. If you respond, you can confirm what they are accusing you of. Answering such a question with a question can thwart their personal attack.

5. *Use a Story to Get Your Point across Gently*

The leaders condemned Jesus for letting a prostitute sit at his feet crying, washing his feet with her tears, and anointing them with perfume. *Jesus told them a story* that honored the woman for showing much love because she received much forgiveness. He then confronted the Pharisees for showing little love because they had received little forgiveness (Luke 7:36-50).

They slandered Jesus for accepting and eating with sinners, so *he told them parables* that highlighted God's grace for the lost (Luke 15).

Again, usually when we engage toxic people, we are trying to vindicate ourselves and convict the aggressor. Since the emotions are already charged, our ability to think rationally is limited. Using stories can help restore rationality and lessen emotional unreasonableness.

6. *Be Prepared to Speak the Truth in Love*

The religious leaders badgered Jesus on the issue of divorce in an attempt to make him look bad: "Is it lawful for a man to divorce his wife for any and every reason?" Jesus reminded them of the sacredness of God's original plan for oneness in marriage and then *confronted them for mistreating women* (Matt 19:1-9).

The Pharisees questioned Jesus in an illegal trial, spat in his face, punched him, slapped him, and mocked him as a helpless prophet. Jesus *silently accepted* their mistreatment. Then he *calmly confronted them* for ganging up on him secretly and for abusing him when he had done nothing wrong (Matt 26:57-67; John 18:19-24).

7. *Forgive*

The crowds watched Jesus being crucified, and he responded, "*Father, forgive them*, for they do not know what they are doing." They sneered at him, "He saved others; let him save himself if he is the Christ."

Forgiveness prevents the poison of our enemy's angry arrows piercing our hearts. Joy and forgiveness are our friends. The human condition is bleak, and great evil occurs. Forgiveness is counter to human nature but reflects the glory of God.

8. *Say Nothing*

There are times when silence speaks louder than words. When Jesus was being falsely accused by the chief priests and elders, he did not defend himself, but the text reads that Jesus remained silent. Pilate tried to get Jesus to answer, but Jesus again said nothing.

When engaging toxic people who have one agenda—your personal destruction—silence can be your greatest weapon (Matt 27:12–14).

9. *Give Them Over to God*

It is very tempting to take justice into our own hands. Jesus could have easily saved himself when in peril, having at least seventy-two thousand angels at his disposal (Matt 26:53) and being God himself (John 18:6), but he gave everything into the Father's hands (Luke 22:42; John 19:11). When attacked by dangerous people, we must give them over to God for his justice or mercy; Rom 12:19 reads, "Do not take revenge, my dear friends, but leave room for God's wrath, for it is written: 'It is mine to avenge; I will repay,' says the Lord." Our job is to focus on the cross and the mercies God bestowed on us for our sins. God's responsibility is for justice or mercy.

Conclusion

Toxic people are part of life's journey and must be dealt with in such a way that we experience no further harm while glorifying God. Even Jesus was unable to convince some people to repent. If he could not get them to change, why should we? Sometimes, toxic people are to be dealt with in such a way that they can no longer harm us by forming a boundary around our lives.[14] Other times, we must endure suffering like Jesus did on the cross and ask God, on their behalf, for their forgiveness (Luke 23:43). We need God's wisdom (Jas 1:5). Regardless of how we respond to them, we know that God can and is using them for his purposes, mainly for our

---

14. A great resource is Cloud and Townsend, *Boundaries*.

holiness. Furthermore, he used toxic people to emancipate creation. If God used toxic people to redeem the world through Jesus, he can use them in our lives, too. This will not be the last time Jesus had to deal with them. We will see more in later chapters.

Questions for Discussion and Personal Reflection

Why is it important to love our enemies and pray for those who persecute us?

1. Why do you think people are so easily threatened?
2. Has there ever been a time when you tried to win someone over who would never forgive you? Do you know of anyone in this type of situation?
3. Are there any toxic people in your life today? How can Jesus's example help you deal with them?
4. Were there ever any people you thought at first were safe but who later became toxic?
5. How can actively forgiving them while placing them in God's hands help us deal with the hurt? Read Rom 12:19 and discuss how this can be applied.
6. Why are toxic people used for our holiness (see also Matt 5:43–48)?

7

Hail to the King

Day Three
Sunday
March 29
AD 33

Mark 11:1-11
Matthew 21:1-9
Luke 19:29-44
John 12:12-15

Christianity is the story of how the rightful King has landed, you might say in disguise, and is calling us all to take part in His great campaign of sabotage.

—C.S. LEWIS

Behold, your King is coming to you.

—ZECHARIAH 9:9

SUNDAY HAS ARRIVED, THE beginning of what today is known as Passion Week. Jesus will awake and have breakfast. Martha is probably up, most likely the first person out of bed to prepare everything for her guests. Breakfast will likely be bread, olives and whatever fruit or vegetable is in season, but this morning carries much more significance for Martha than just a meal.

Thoughts of the evening before, where she hosted a celebratory feast for Jesus, may have been at the forefront of her mind. Jesus most likely told her about the week ahead. Martha knew her dear friend would face the most trying and important week of his life. She is probably thinking of his words as she prepares breakfast and most pronounced would be his declaration of death and resurrection. When Jesus is buried six days later, Martha will remember how she doubted her friend after her brother had lain in a tomb for four days (John 11:17-27, 38-39) and remember how her brother walked out of the tomb back into her life (John 11:40-44). Recollections of Jesus's past miracles will sooth this Sunday morning anxiety, and she will joyfully serve her guests a morning meal.

It is uncertain whether or not Mary is awake this morning but six days from this morning, she will be. When news of Jesus's crucifixion reaches her, she will cry but then look at the alabaster jar she used to anoint her friend's head and feet (Mark 14:3-9; Matt 26:6-13; John 12:3-8) recalling his words of resurrection and work of raising her brother from the dead. She will smell the fragrance of the perfume she anointed Jesus with (John 12:3) and be comforted.[1] Her friend and Lord will not be gone for long.

During breakfast, when discussing the trials of the week, Lazarus is least troubled; Jesus himself had raised him from the dead. When Jesus talked about his death and resurrection at the Saturday evening meal and Sunday morning breakfast, Lazarus will be totally at ease. He himself had already experienced death and is not in the least worried for his friend. But Jesus will give Lazarus instructions to remain in Bethany and not follow him to Jerusalem. Lazarus wants to be in Jerusalem for Jesus but knows it is too risky. Part of Jesus's mission is to die for the sins of humanity and then rise. Next Sunday, Jesus will follow Lazarus returning from the dead. No one knows this better than the Messiah's friend, who had been in a grave not too long ago. Lazarus knows Jesus will not have a lengthy stay, shorter than his burial stopover. He may even exchange a resurrection story with Jesus about what it is like to be dead. When Jesus dies, Lazarus will exhort his sisters not to worry much and remind them of how Jesus brought him back from the grave.

Jesus's friends want to be with their Lord during this week but they know they cannot be. For one, Jesus will need a place to stay during Passion Week and will return each night to Bethany until Thursday. Another reason is that Lazarus is also a target of the Jewish religious leaders (John 12:9–11); because Jesus raised him from the dead after four days, even more people began to follow him. The Bethany beloved will stay behind.

Jesus knew his disciples would not be very supportive during his greatest hours of need but time with the Bethany beloved would fill the Lord's heart. He has spent Friday evening, Saturday, and the beginning of Sunday in Bethany and now is ready to be crowned as Israel's final king.

Headed toward the Holy City

Jesus and his disciples have now finished their breakfast and are headed toward Jerusalem, about two miles away. Crowds of people know Jesus is staying in Bethany because they saw him the night before. Adherents in this crowd witnessed Jesus's miracle of raising Lazarus (John 12:9); now they are here to see if this miracle man is indeed the prophesied king of Israel.

---

1. We will delve deeper into this issue in a coming chapter.

When Jesus leaves the house, crowds begin to follow. A few will see Jesus leave and begin to inform others. While the crowd slowly forms, Jesus told them he was headed to Jerusalem. That would mean one thing to the mind of the Jew: King David has arrived!

Jericho and the Messiah

There may have been people as far away as Jericho present, about thirteen to fourteen miles from Bethany. Lazarus was not the only miracle recently performed. When Jesus left Ephraim en route to Jerusalem, he healed a man by the name of Bartimaeus and his companion who were blind in the vicinity of Jericho (Mark 10:46–52; Matt 20:29–34; Luke 18:35–43).

Matthew and Mark place this miracle just before Jesus's triumphal entry into Jerusalem. Why would the writers place this incident here? When John the Baptist was in prison, just before his beheading, he questioned whether or not his relative was the Messiah (Matt 11:2–19; Luke 7:18–35). Disappointed and discouraged while awaiting death, John sent some of his disciples to Jesus asking him, "Are You the Expected One, or shall we look for someone else?" (Matt 11:3; Luke 7:19). The first thing Jesus told John's disciples to tell the Baptist was that the blind receive sight (Luke 7:22; Matt 11:5).

Luke adds the story of Zacchaeus in Luke 19:1–10 to draw attention to the fact of the poor hearing the good news, the last observation of Jesus's answer to John the Baptist (Luke 7:22; Matt 11:5).[2] The writers are communicating that Jesus is indeed the Expected One John was looking for and found, fulfilling the prophesies of the coming Messiah.

The writer of Mark records an earlier healing of a blind person in Bethsaida (Mark 8:22–26). Just like the healing of Bartimaeus, there is a declaration of Jesus's messianic mantle of the blind receiving sight (Mark 8:27–30; 10:47–48; 11:1–11).[3] It would not be a surprise to see the healing of the blind men in the Jericho district cause its people to believe Messiah had come.

Jesus may be reenacting Joshua's march into the promised land with the first area that Israel encountered being Jericho. Joshua took the city after seven days and his name is the Hebrew form of Jesus; hence, the Jericho reference before Jerusalem.

---

2. Luke 19:11–27 continues the Jericho narrative. On the Old Testament reference of the poor hearing the good news, Isa 29:18, 19; 61:1, 2; cf. Luke 4:18.

3. The first use of the messianic title "Son of David" in Mark is found in 10:47–48. The only other time it is used in Mark is in 12:35 but it is not used in reference to Jesus. For "Son of David" as a messianic title, see Isa 11:1–2; Jer 23:5–6; Ezek 34:23–24.

Perhaps the palm branches that will be laid on the path during Jesus's ride into Jerusalem are people from Jericho (John 12:13). Palm branches are not believed to be native to Jerusalem but may have been in Jericho. Just as there is a Bethany following, the healing of the two blind beggars in the vicinity of Jericho could have inspired more followers. Jericho Jews would be in the Jerusalem region for the Passover celebration and may have brought palm branches in anticipation of Messiah's coming. Jesus knows these crowds are enamored by his miracle working and does nothing to dissuade them from believing he is the Messiah of Israel.

At the Halfway Point

Jesus is on his way to Jerusalem to claim his right as the monarch. He has now traveled about a mile and has reached Bethphage, also known as the "house of figs." He knows that he is the fulfillment of the Davidic Covenant found in 2 Sam 7:11–16 and approaches Jerusalem as its king.

It has been almost six hundred and forty years since the nation had a physical king. Zedekiah was installed as the king of Judah by the Babylonians between 606–597 BC.[4] After Zedekiah tried to rebel against Nebuchadnezzar, the Babylonians removed him from the kingship and appointed a governor named Gedalaih who was later assassinated by Judeans.[5] But as far as the kingship, Zedekiah was the last. The northern kingdom of Israel, consisting of ten out of the twelve tribes, had already been in captivity since 722 BC by Assyria.[6]

Almost six hundred and forty years later, after centuries of being ruled by the likes of the Babylonians, Persians, Greeks, and now Rome, Jesus will ride into Jerusalem as the last king of Israel (Luke 1:30–33). At a time when the Roman government was oppressing Israel with heavy taxes, influencing Judaic culture, and imposing civic/imperial cults worshipping the emperor, great poverty existed over the Jewish people who still had to tithe and offer sacrifices to the temple. Jesus's coming offered the nation great hope that a king as great as David would lead the military of Israel over Roman rule. Though he will fulfill the covenant God made with David in 2 Sam 7:11–16

---

4. The exact dates are disputed among scholars but these two dates correspond with cycles of the Babylonian captivity.

5. See Dearman, *Jeremiah, Lamentations*, 31–32.

6. The last king of the northern kingdom would have been Hoshea who reigned from 732–722 BC.

where someone from the house of David will sit on the throne of Israel forever, Jesus's first coming as king is mainly to act as Isaiah's Suffering Servant (Isa 52:13—53:12). Jesus will sit on this throne forever (Luke 1:31–33), but before he sits on the throne, he will sit on a young donkey.

The Colt and Cloaks

Progress is being made on the Jerusalem journey; Bethany and Bethphage are now behind. His disciples have found a colt and its mother in the village, laid their cloaks on the colt and left Bethphage, less than a mile from Jerusalem (Matt 21:1–7; Mark 11:4–7; Luke 19:32–37).[7]

We know from Matthew and John's Gospels that Jesus is fulfilling Zech 9:9 in riding the colt (Matt 21:5; John 12:15),[8] but another aspect of Jesus's riding on the colt would signal to the Jewish people that David's replacement is coming. In 1 Kgs 1:30–34, Solomon will succeed his father David as king and one act Solomon performs is to ride David's mule. This is a public proclamation that Solomon's rule is under David's personal blessing.[9] Now Jesus will ride a colt that has never been ridden into Jerusalem. When the Jews see Jesus on the colt, they will associate Jesus as the Davidic king they have been expecting for over six hundred years.[10]

The disciples' request of the colt in Bethphage goes smoothly without squabbling from the owner. Their reason for borrowing the colt: "The Lord has need of it." The owner would link this with Jesus and freely offer his foal. Someday he will boast of this animal as the one on which sat the everlasting King.

Now Jesus has his colt and sits, less than a mile from the temple. As the colt moves out of Bethphage, the crowds are spreading their cloaks on the ground thereby communicating to the world that Jewish royalty has arrived. In 2 Kgs 9:1–13, Jehu, son of Jehoshaphat, is abruptly anointed as

---

7. Specifically at this point, they are about one kilometer or 5/8 of a mile from the temple. This information was provided by distinguished professor of the New Testament from St. John's Nottingham Dr. Stephen Travis via e-mail correspondence.

8. Donahue and Harrington, *Gospel of Mark*, 321, write: "The OT background of Jesus's symbolic action is the description of the divine warrior in Zech 9:9. . . . Matthew (in 21:2, 7) envisions the presence of two animals—the donkey and her colt—on the basis of an excessively literal reading of Zech 9:9."

9. See also Gen 41:41–44 and Esth 6:7–9 for similar scenarios of leadership blessing.

10. Donahue and Harrington, *Mark*, 317, write, "The son of David par excellence was Solomon, and in NT times Solomon was frequently portrayed as a . . . healer."

king by a prophet. After Jehu told his fellow officers that a prophet anointed him as king, they immediately spread their cloaks under Jehu to acknowledge their new monarch. Jesus is receiving the same royal treatment; the act of him "stepping" over the cloaks is a sign the anointed king over Israel has arrived.

The word in the original language for cloak is the same for garment or clothes. As the crowds are spreading their garments for the king to ride over, six days from now on Good Friday, the Roman soldiers will divide Jesus's garments among themselves. It was Jesus's garment that brought healing to a woman who was hemorrhaging for twelve years. She said to herself that if she could touch Jesus's garment, she would be healed (Luke 8:43–44). Her faith made her well.

One act blind Bartimaeus performed before his healing was to throw off his "cloak."[11] The next time Mark writes about cloaks and garments being taken off is now,[12] today, Sunday, Jesus is entering Jerusalem from the Mountain of Olives, less than a mile from the temple. Crowds are spreading their outfits on the ground as homage to their king.

Almost There

People have been talking about Jesus since the Passover feast began (John 11:54ff.). His recent miracles, coupled with three to three and half years of ministry, has built a notable reputation. During this time, the Jewish religious leaders became aware of him, knowing works like healing and resurrection. They knew of the lepers being cleansed and the blind receiving sight, yet for nearly three years, they refused to turn from their ways to worship. Instead, they tried to remove him. Now Jesus was riding on a colt nearing Jerusalem to the cheers of crowds, riding on a path of leaves, branches and cloaks, accepting the praise of Messiah. The Jewish leaders have a choice: worship or war. There are no other options, Jesus has

---

11. Boring, *Mark*, 306, writes, "By throwing off his cloak aside, Bartimaeus threw off the garment of his old self and the life he had been living in blindness, beside the way rather than on it." Many others have a similar comment to Bartimaeus discarding his cloak/garment but given that this is the only reference to Jesus in Mark as "Son of David" and the triumphal entry pericope immediately follows, the removal of the cloak could also carry a messianic/royal significance.

12. Boring, *Mark*, 306, writes, "Throughout Mark, clothing is often symbolic of the significance of the person, and, like the name, partakes of the reality of the person behind himself or herself (cf. 1:6; 5:27; 6:9; 9:3; 11:7; 14:51)."

intensified the situation and people are following. Do the leaders join the crowds in welcoming Messiah? Or do they try to vanquish him? Six days from now, they will nail Jesus on a cross believing they have won but God will use this to orchestrate a final victory, not just over the leaders, but over all: cosmic and worldly (Col 1:13–20).

In Jerusalem

Before Jesus rides through Jerusalem's gates, he will weep over the city, knowing they will reject him and unrelentingly punish (Luke 19:41–44). This rejection will lead to the downfall of the city (Luke 19:44). Jesus still proceeds, knowing that Jerusalem must endure their personal affliction before redemption; because of Golgotha, Jesus will be able to make Jerusalem the city after his own heart.

His entry was such that the whole city stirred. Some were not aware that Jesus was coming and asked, "Who is this person causing so much commotion?" Others were explaining that it was Jesus, the prophet from Nazareth (Matt 21:10–11). The king has now entered, accepting the people's praise and will head back to Bethany to spend the night with his friends. Great joy, exuberance, and jubilation are occurring as the people shout their praises to the Lord.

In the past, it was not uncommon for Jesus to request silence.[13] With his miracles drawing messianic attention, there was the possibility his works would precipitate a calamity that would hinder his mission and ministry from being completed in God's timing. People may have tried to coronate him as king too soon. Silence was key early on. When silence was not honored, Jesus's work was altered (e.g., Mark 1:45).

Christ's ministry would endure over three years and the Father had his timing for all events. Jesus knew he could assume the throne of Israel early on but asked for silence among those who believed he was a ruler. It was not time yet. His disciples would need to understand and then carry on his mission when he went back to heaven. Their training was not complete.

But today things are different, the time has arrived and this Sunday, Jesus is not asking for silence, the Pharisees will (Luke 19:39). They think

---

13. This theme is especially pronounced in the book of Mark where scholars have referred to Jesus not trying to draw attention to himself as the "Messianic Secret." Jesus asks his disciples, people and even demons to remain silent about Jesus's identity and works; see Mark 1:34, 44; 3:11–12; 5:42–43; 7:36; 8:26, 30; 9:9–10.

they will eventually silence Jesus on the cross but end up only perpetuating his dominion until the day of his return (Acts 1:11).

Before he returns to Bethany, he will first enter the temple courts before leaving (Mark 11:11). David had the vision to build the temple, Solomon, his son, built it after seven years of construction, and Jesus will return to Jerusalem tomorrow to cleanse it. The temple had become a place of business instead of adoration. Day three saw Jesus end the silence of his royalty by entering the holy city as the fulfillment of the Davidic covenant. Tomorrow, his first act will be to cleanse the temple, the Jews most precious domain.

Questions for Discussion and Personal Reflection

When you think of Jesus, is he more of a friend to you or is he king?

1. How can seeing Jesus as the king affect our daily life?
2. Many followed Jesus because of the miraculous works he did; what great works has Jesus done in your life?
3. How can meditating on God's faithfulness in the past help us live in the future?
4. How can we make Jesus more "King" in our life?

8

The Monday Temple Cleansing

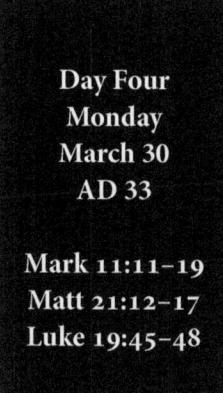

Day Four
Monday
March 30
AD 33

Mark 11:11–19
Matt 21:12–17
Luke 19:45–48

And here, shipmates, is true and faithful repentance; not clamorous for pardon, but grateful for punishment.

—HERMAN MELVILLE

All this took place because the Israelites had sinned against the LORD their God. . . . So the LORD was very angry with Israel and removed them from his presence.

—2 KINGS 17:7, 18

LIFE HAS DISTRACTIONS. MANY can become too focused on things that are good but not best. Things like jobs, grades, wealth, and personal reputation can overwhelm our priorities, crowding out what is most important: loving God and people.

Life has lustration, a process leading to purification. Lustration can help take our attention off of secondary self-glorifying pursuits, reorienting back to what is most important. Since God disciplines those he loves (Heb 12:6), cleansing and purification will occur, rescuing the heart from an overzealous appetite for greed, ambition, prominence, reputation, and fame.

The last resort is the instrument of devastation, precisely what will happen in Israel's future.[1] Jesus's Monday cleansing of the temple is a precursor to its AD 70 destruction, a little while afterwards, Israel again will be scattered.[2]

---

1. Telford, *Temple and Tree*, 238, writes, "The tree's lack of response and its subsequent withering could be seen as a solemn, proleptic sign that judgment had been pronounced on the Temple, and that this judgment had finally been consummated in the eschatological events of 70 CE."

2. This is the view of most scholars that the overall message of the section of Mark 11:12–25 is in regards to the future destruction of Israel and the temple. For a good survey of various interpretations of the pericope, see Collins, *Mark*, 522–37.

Sunday: The Day Before

Yesterday, Jesus entered Jerusalem to the chorus of a king's welcome. Once he entered the city, he proceeded to the temple (Mark 11:11). Before entering, Jesus's heart was burdened (Luke 19:41).[3] Knowing that the nation had declined and would eventually require purification; great suffering was ahead (Luke 19:44). Though Jesus knew the temple and the city would face punishment, entering the temple area on Sunday was not easy. Jesus knew something was seriously wrong and his first order of business when he appeared this Monday would be to make things right.

Sunday night was probably spent describing to Mary, Martha, and Lazarus the day's happenings and the condition of the temple.[4] Sleep would be sparse and Jesus may have not slept at all, spending the night in prayer (cf. Luke 6:12), but this will not deter him from making the temple a place where his Father would approve. This would not be the first time Jesus had to purify the temple.[5] Two to three years earlier, he had visited Jerusalem

---

3. Telford, *Temple and Tree*, 239, believes the writer of Luke felt this scene was too harsh and omitted it from his gospel. Telford writes, "The harsh import of Mark's story was recognized by Luke who decided to omit it. The third evangelist replaced the pericope with a characteristic lament for Jerusalem and earlier has Jesus recount a parable of a barren fig-tree to which a period of grace was granted." It may not be the "harshness" that made Luke omit this. His audience was not mainly Jewish and as I will argue later, this scene, which all four Gospels touch on, may not have suited Luke's readers. I will later argue that Jesus cursing of the fig tree is in reference to Jer 8:13—9:23 which is the Haftarah read on the morning of the Ninth of Ab commemorating the Jewish fast—Tisha B'Av—possibly the solemnest holiday on the Jewish calendar remembering the destruction of the temple in 586 BC and AD 70. There is evidence from Zech 8:19 that this fast may have been celebrated during the postexilic period.

4. The issue of the temple being overly dependent for piety in Judaism has been a subject addressed by biblical authors (cf. Matt 12:6; 26:57–64; 27:40). See also Hamm, *Talmid Service in Luke-Acts*, 65. Grabbe, *Second Temple Judaism*, 40–41, writes,

> The main religious institution was the Jerusalem temple, and temple worship went back many centuries in Jewish and Israelite history. The temple was not the same as a synagogue. The main activity in the temple was blood sacrifice.... The emphasis on blood sacrifice should not be misconstrued, as abhorrent as the practice may seem to some. It was not "empty ritual" as so often portrayed in prejudiced Christian (usually Protestant) propaganda. On the contrary, the sacrificial ritual was suffused with deep religious symbolism. This symbolism was taken up into later Judaism, after the cessation of the temple cult, and into Christianity.

5. Scholars are not in agreement here. Some hold to two temple cleansings while others hold to one incident that John's writer simply moves to a different place in order to communicate his message. Many hold to one temple cleanse like Keener, *Gospel of John*, 518, who writes, "John adapts the more familiar chronology of the passion tradition to

and performed a similar temple cleanse (John 2:14–17),[6] having made a whip to chase out the moneychangers and businessmen.[7] Now, he will do it again.

Christ the Curser?

Jesus is up early this Monday morning,[8] and wakes his disciples so they can make the two-mile trek to Jerusalem. During this Passion Week, the temple will be a central place where he teaches during the day and performs selected healings (Luke 19:47, Matt 21:14), but the Lord cannot teach in "a

---

make an important point." If there is only one temple cleansing, then the issue of chronology arises. John places his cleansing early in Jesus ministry; while the Synoptics places their accounts during Passion Week. Brown, *Gospel according to John*, 117ff., discusses the issue of chronology between John's and the Synoptics presuming there was only one temple cleansing. Others hold to two temple cleansings like Bock, *Luke*, 1576–77, and Morris, *Gospel according to John*, 190, who writes, "But in view of the major differences in wording and in setting, as well as in time, we will require more evidence than a facile assumption that two similar narratives must refer to the same event. The words in common are very few, "sellers," "tables," "doves," "moneychangers," and without them it would be practically impossible to tell a story of temple-cleansing." Morris, *Gospel according to John*, 190–91, goes on to write:

> Moreover, the evil in question was one which was likely to recur after a check. Jesus's action, though salutary is not likely to have put a permanent end to the practice. Nor can it be said that the authorities would certainly have taken such action after one incident as would effectively prevent a recurrence. At the time indicated in John Jesus was quite unknown. His strong action would have aroused a furor in Jerusalem, but that is all. The authorities may well have been disinclined to go to extremes against Him, especially if there was some public feeling against the practices He opposed. It was quite otherwise at the time indicated in Mark. Then Jesus was well known and vigorously opposed by the high-priestly party. His action would inevitably lead to strong counter-action.

For a good summary of the temple-cleansing scene of the Synoptics with John, see Bock, *Luke*, 1576.

6. The book of John specifically mentions three Passovers but in John 5:1 there is reference to another Jewish feast, which could have been a fourth Passover. John also mentions the feast of Tabernacles (7:2) and Dedication/Hanukkah (10:22). Many scholars hold to the fact that there was only one temple cleanse; therefore, John is using the same scene for theological reasons. On the issue of Jesus cleansing the temple twice, see Chapple, *Jesus' Intervention in the Temple*, 545–69, where he argues that the temple cleansing scene in John is not the same as the Synoptic accounts.

7. See Morris, *Gospel according to John*, 191.

8. See also Painter, *Mark's Gospel*, 156–57.

den of robbers," and is about to drive them out and restore "the house of prayer" (Jer 7:11; Isa 56:7).[9]

Because he is up so early, Martha is probably still asleep and cannot provide breakfast. She undoubtedly stayed up late Sunday night to hear Jesus describe the day's events and knows that the condition of the temple was on her friend's heart. Her spirit wants to wake but is too tired from staying up late, and worn out from the energy hospitality required. Jesus and his disciples had already lodged for four days.

The group of thirteen arises and leaves for Jerusalem. Almost a mile into the journey, Jesus becomes hungry (Mark 11:12) and sees a fig tree bearing leaves.[10] Knowing figs are not in season,[11] Jesus does not want to waste this opportunity to teach his disciples a valuable lesson. When Jesus finds out there are not figs on the tree, he curses it, acting out of character.[12] It appears Jesus is mistreating the tree, angry because of hunger, lashing out by abusing his powers of deity on an innocent shrub.

When people think of Jesus, they think of someone full of love, joy and grace, not one who takes out his anger and unleashes his power on a poor defenseless fig tree that he knows is not in season for fruit.[13] His power is usually used for good, not anger. Even demons that possess humans are shown a degree of mercy (see Mark 5:1–20; Matt 8:28–34; Luke 8:26–37). The dead are raised, the sick are healed, the blind see, demons are cast out, close to twenty thousand people are fed,[14] and Gentiles are saved, but a

---

9. Kirk, *Time for Figs*, 509–27. Kirk writes, "Not only does the fig-tree narrative interpret the temple-clearing incident, but the teaching in 11:17 (Mark) that invokes Israel's prophets substantiates the temple-judgment narrative, and the teaching on prayer establishes the community as God's eschatological replacement to that physical place of prayer and forgiveness" (527).

10. See appendix 2 for a more detailed discussion of the cursing of the fig tree scene.

11. Much discussion has been made about the Greek word for time/season: kairo,j. For a few discussions, see France, *Gospel of Mark*, 439–41; BDAG 497–99; Lohmeyer, *Das Evangelium des Markus*, 234; Hiers, *Not the Season*, 394–400; Cotter, "For It Was Not the Season," 62–66; Telford, *More Fruit*, 264–304; Collins, *Mark*, 526n32; Oakman, *Cursing Fig Trees*, 256–57.

12. Most commentators appeal to theological teaching in exonerating Jesus's behavior. France, *Gospel of Mark*, 439, is not so kind: "It is hard to imagine why Jesus should have misused his miraculous power in this petty way, and still harder to understand why anyone should record it." France goes on to write, "It should have been possible to find a more wholesome narrative basis for the lessons on the power of faith which both Matthew and Mark have seen fit to draw from the story."

13. See France, *Gospel of Mark*, 439.

14. The Bible states that there are five thousand fed but this would only include men,

The Monday Temple Cleansing

poor defenseless tree that by the next day will be withered to its roots (Mark 11:20), this does not sound like the Jesus we know.

But the disciples will not be surprised when this happens. They probably understood Jeremiah 8—9 where the temple is denounced; they will know that the Lord declares, "There will be no figs on the tree, and their leaves will wither. What I have given them will be taken from them" (Jer 8:13).

Jeremiah 8:13 is part of a larger section of 8:13—9:23.[15] The Jewish religion reads Jer 8:13—9:23 on their holiday (fast)—Tisha B'Av—which commemorates and remembers the destruction of the temple by the Babylonians and is considered the most solemn day of the Jewish calendar.[16] By withering of the cursed fig tree, the disciples could have associated the Jeremiah pericope with the temple being destroyed again, but Jesus is greater than the temple (Matt 12:1–6).[17]

What gets lost in focusing too much on Jesus's actions against the fig tree is the latter part of Mark 11:14: "His disciples heard him."[18] Jesus is using this action against the tree as a means of preparation.[19] Knowing his time on earth is limited—Jesus will die in five days, rise three days later and ascend back to heaven in forty-five—his final preparations are necessary to instill lessons to help his disciples withstand the trials they will face after Jesus returns to heaven. No greater trial will be experienced than the pummeling of the nation accompanied by the destruction of their beloved house of worship.

---

making the number fed much higher: Mark 6:30-44; Matt 14:13-21; Luke 9:10-17; John 6:5-13.

15. On the issue of the New Testament being influenced by Jewish lectionaries, see Guilding, *Fourth Gospel*. See also a response by Morris, *Jewish Lectionaries*. Collins, *Mark*, 525n28, does mention the pericope in terms of Jer 8:8-13 and the indictment against the leaders.

16. Today, it also commemorates the destruction of Herod's temple in AD 70 almost exactly 657 years apart. History records that the temples were destroyed in 586/587 BC and AD 70 on the same day, the ninth of Ab. For the notion of Tisha B'Av celebrated during New Testament time see Gelardini, *Hebrews*, 107-24.

17. Not all are in agreement that the destruction of the temple is what is being alluded to. Collins, *Mark*, 526, holds to the reference referring to "the culpability of the leaders." See Telford, *Temple and Tree*, 1-25, for a summary of the various references to the pericope up to 1980.

18. E.g., France, *Gospel of Mark*, 443, describes the mention of "his disciples hearing" as "redundant . . . in order to establish his point."

19. Gray, *Temple in Mark*, 39-41, argues that Mark's purpose for the disciples hearing was for discernment. Whether or not they understood right then and there is uncertain.

The twelve are about to witness Jesus cleansing the temple after cursing the fig tree.[20] They should know the fig tree represents Israel (Luke 13:6–9) and will associate the temple with the fig tree facing destruction.[21] Most of these men will not be alive when Rome destroys the temple in AD 70, only John the beloved disciple will remain. But most of these men will live around thirty years after Jesus ascends to heaven and though most will not see the temple destroyed, their disciples will and they need to prepare them for the heart of the nation to be ripped out.

At the center of Jewish life was the temple, and the religious leaders had allowed it to become a place of profit instead of purity.[22] When the temple is destroyed, the life of Judaism will be decimated.[23] The disciples of Jesus who believe Jesus is greater than the temple—which will include second-generation disciples—will be the ones to help many disgruntled and hopeless people through their darkest moment.[24] By cursing the fig

---

20. Boring, *Mark*, 319, writes, "The fig tree seems to represent the temple: its leaves, notable from a distance, give it an impressive appearance (cf. 13:1–3). Jesus approaches to inspect it, looking for fruit, as he had inspected the temple (v. 11). Like Yahweh seeking fruit from Israel, Jesus is disappointed (cf. Jer 8:13; Joel 1:7; Ezek 17:24; Mic 7:1, Hs 9:10, 16–17)."

21. But they may not discern this teaching during Jesus's time, see Gray, *Temple in Mark*, 39–41. On the fig tree symbolizing the people or God and their obedience, see France, *Gospel of Mark*, 439. Also, King, *Jeremiah*, 148, writes, "The destruction of fig trees was one of the signs of pending economic catastrophe." King goes on to write, "Jeremiah's vision of two baskets of figs placed before the Temple (24:1–10) is well known.... The good figs symbolize those Judahites exiled to Babylon in 597 B.C.E., who would turn to the Lord in repentance and would be returned to Judah. The bad figs represent those ... remaining in Jerusalem in 597 B.C.E., who resisted Nebuchadnezzar and were unrepentant; they would be rejected." For Old Testament references of the fig tree representing Israel and the temple, see Hos 9:10, 16–17; Mic 4:4; 7:1; Jer 8:13; 24:1–10; 29:17; Joel 1:7, 12; Zech 14; Ezek 17;47, and Telford, *Temple and Tree*, 128–75.

22. Boring, *Mark*, 319, writes, "Like the prophets of Israel, Jesus pronounces God's judgment on the unfruitful tree. That no one is to eat fruit from it forever shows that the pronouncement represents the ultimate, eschatological judgment of God, not a relative, temporary punishment. So also the withering from the roots up (v. 20) shows the utter devastation of the tree, which, representing the temple, is destroyed and will not recover."

23. France, *Gospel of Mark*, 436–37, writes, "The temple was not only the heart of Israel's religious life but also the symbol of its national identity.... The patriotic as well as religious symbolism of the temple was thus enormous, and the magnificence of Herod's rebuilding matched its symbolic significance."

24. France writes, "But with hindsight it could be seen ... as the beginning of an increasingly explicit campaign against what the temple now stood for, the first demonstration of judgment which must ultimately lead to the total dissolution of the building itself." France goes on to write, "Mark, by associating Jesus's action with the cursing of the fig tree,

The Monday Temple Cleansing

tree—which the disciples will see the next day has been withered[25]—Jesus is using a powerful example to teach his followers the future demise of the temple and the nation.

Cleansing the Temple for Prayer and Ministry

Jesus headed to the temple. The next thing his disciples will witness is their master driving out the moneychangers and businessmen (Mark 11:15–17).[26] He knew from being in the temple on Sunday that it had declined into a place unworthy of worship.

Passivity will be nonexistent; with great fervor for his Father, Jesus purges the temple court.[27] No longer will there be short cuts for businessmen to transport goods (Mark 11:16), no longer will money be primary over prayer; the dross is removed from his Father's house.[28]

When Jesus performs this act on Monday, the Jewish religious leaders will consider this a major attack, heightening their already fervent desire to destroy him (Mark 11:18; Matt 21:15; Luke 19:47–48).[29] Matthew records Jesus's works and praise from children, causing the leaders to become more indignant (Matt 21:15).[30] Protected by his popularity, Jesus is able to continue his temple teaching and healing (Mark 11:18; Matt 21:13–16; Luke 19:47–48).

They (religious leaders) should have been the ones who protected the purity of the temple but it was they who allowed the temple courts to be a place of trade when God's intent was for it to be a place of adoration.

Not only did the religious leaders stand to lose profit from the moneychangers and businessmen being removed, Jesus cleansing the temple by ceasing commerce was a threat to their authority. They even asked Jesus

---

ensures that his readers see it in this wider and more ominous perspective" (ibid., 437).

25. See Telford, *Temple and Tree*.

26. This would be the Court of the Gentiles in the outer area of the temple where anyone was granted access just outside of the Beautiful Gate.

27. France, *Gospel of Matthew*, 783, writes, "The setting is the Court of the Gentiles."

28. France argues that Jesus's anger is not necessarily directed at the business people but the Sadducee establishment that allowed the temple to become a place of commerce (ibid., 784).

29. See Bock, *Luke*, 1580, where he notes the unique grouping of the chief priests, scribes, and leader of the people. Bock writes, "Mark mentions only the chief priests and scribes, so that Luke draws a slightly wider circle of blame."

30. See also France, *Gospel of Matthew*, 788–89.

how he received this authority to kick out the business people when they were the ones in charge of the temple (Mark 11:27–33; Matt 21:23–27; Luke 20:1–8). Not appreciating having their authority usurped;[31] despite being the ones who allowed the temple court become a place of profit over prayer,[32] they did nothing to thwart the Messiah.

Jesus saw this for what it was: a corruption of his Father's house. The pride of power and the greed of profit blinded the religious leaders to the fact that the temple, a place of worship, repentance and prayer had become a place for monetary gain.

Destined for Doom

Leadership is destiny. After Jesus purges the temple of commerce, he performs miracles of healing (Matt 21:14) and teaches (Luke 19:47), all to the chagrin of the Jewish leaders (Matt 21:14; Luke 19:48). Because these men failed to repent, they will soon lead the nation through a maelstrom of destruction.[33]

This Monday, Jesus enters the temple; restoration is his plan. When the disciples see the fig tree the next day (Mark 11:20), it will be completely withered to the roots. His disciples will remember the cursing before and discuss the event. Rather than affirming their observation, Jesus finalizes his teaching on the coming destruction of the temple and scattering of the nation, but the power of prayer will not be mitigated without the temple. Not only would prayer outside the temple be powerful but also, employing hyperbole, Jesus says their prayers can move the mountain that the temple is built upon.[34]

---

31. Bock, *Luke*, 1582, lists five controversies between Jesus and the leaders in the pericope of Luke 20:1–8: source of authority (20:1–8); parable of vineyard (20:9–19); Caesar's tax (20:20–26); resurrection and Sadducees (20:27–40), and Ps 110 (20:41–44). Luke omits the fig tree narrative.

32. Marshall, *Faith in Mark's Narrative*, 162, writes, "Its rulers have comprehensively failed to make it a genuine house of prayer, worthy of God's eschatological designs for the nations.... By becoming a den of thieves and practicing an exploitative and hypocritical piety, the Jerusalem temple has disqualified itself as the place where Isaiah's prophecy shall be fulfilled."

33. Boring, *Mark*, 320, writes, "But the temple in flames meant that both temple and faith had to be rethought. Both Jew's and Christians were refashioning their faith and theology in the light of the temple's destruction."

34. Some hold the mountain to be the Mt. of Olives. If they were in Bethphage, then they would have just exited the mountain, but since the temple was such a strong

The Monday Temple Cleansing

Jesus uses his cursing of the fig tree and cleansing of the temple as preparation for his disciples—present and future—for the coming calamity of Israel. It will be necessary for the future redemption of God's chosen people to suffer centuries of oppression from foreign nations or else the Jewish nation would be spiritually lost for eternity. In our own lives, God uses times of discipline and suffering to purify us so we can be more like Jesus and get our lives back on track according to his word. The suffering soul is one that is being sanctified.

Questions for Discussion and Personal Reflection

Has there been a time in your life where you have strayed far from your faith? How were you restored?

1. What causes people to disobey God?
2. Are there areas in your life that need cleansing?
3. How has Jesus performed a "temple cleansing" in your life?
4. What are some creative ways to read, study, pray, and mediate on the Bible?
5. What are things in your life that distract you from prayer and worship?

---

teaching point, this could have been the mountain of reference. See Keener, *Commentary on the Gospel of Matthew*, 505.

Sanhedrin Stress and Story Time

9

> When dealing with people, remember you are not dealing with creatures of logic, but creatures of emotion.
>
> —DALE CARNEGIE

> A simple rule in dealing with those who are hard to get along with is to remember that this person is striving to assert his superiority; and you must deal with him from that point of view.
>
> —ALFRED ADLER

> Do not answer a fool according to his folly, or you yourself will be just like him.
>
> —PROVERBS 26:4

**Day Five
Tuesday
March 31
AD 33**

Mark 11:20—13:37
Matt 21:23—25:46
Luke 20:1—21:36

TUESDAYS ARE USUALLY SLOWER in modern Western society. Restaurants and businesses often have "deals" to attract consumers. One of the slowest travel days for airliners is Tuesday, which often produces cheaper airfares, but during Passion Week two thousand years ago, Jesus again dealt with opponents who were threatened by his ministry.

Tuesday morning has arrived and Jesus leaves Bethany; after passing the fig tree cursed the day before (Mark 11:20–25) Jesus arrives at the temple to the anticipation of the crowds (Luke 21:37–38).[1] We read in Mark 11:27–33 that while walking in the temple courts, the Lord is met by the

---

1. Craddock, *Luke*, 248–49, compares Luke 21:37–38 with John 7:53—8:2 and writes, "Some manuscripts then follow the story of Jesus and the woman taken into adultery. However, a few manuscripts locate the story after Luke 21:38. One can see by the similarity between Luke 21:37–38 and John 7:53—8:2 how scribes would find Luke a comfortable setting for the story."

chief priests, the teachers of the law and the elders. These men were likely representative of the Sanhedrin: the highest Judaic court during the Roman Empire.[2] In the eyes of the leaders, Jesus has overstepped his authorial boundaries and in effect, "stepped on toes."[3] Having cleansed the temple the day before, much to their vexation, and teaching daily with no official title, the rulers are overwhelmingly sensitive.

It is not surprising the Jewish leaders would question Jesus on the issue of authority; since he had no official standing in the Sanhedrin but acted as if he possessed superior influence; those in power would feel threatened. Christ's high popularity with the crowds shielded him from initial attacks; hence, the need to trick Jesus into arrest. It is clear that this body of men who know Torah (Jewish Written Law, first five books of the Bible) better than anyone was threatened. Christ had no formal education while the leaders would have the best scholarship in Judaic matters. This scene illustrates that titles are not impressive in heaven. Jesus has gained a huge following and is exercising authority that threatens people in command.[4]

Power corrupts the best of persons and despite their superior knowledge of the Scriptures, the Jewish leaders are blind to the fact that the Messiah, prophesied throughout the Tanakh (Old Testament), is standing in their midst. Any one who could irritate Rome also posed a threat to their personal kingdom. The religious leaders had been planning on Jesus's demise long before Passion Week (Mark 3:6). Works of forgiving sins (Mark 2:1–12), eating with sinners and tax collectors (Mark 2:13–17; Matt 9:9–13; Luke 5:27–32), and not honoring the Sabbath (Mark 2:23–27) made Jesus a target.

The plan escalates in Mark 12:13 when members of the Sanhedrin[5] send Pharisees and Herodians in hope of trapping their foe,[6] building up their plan to have him killed. These two groups—Pharisees and Herodi-

---

2. Or at the very least, temple authorities, see Culpepper, *Mark*, 384–85. For this group constituting the Sanhedrin, see Moloney, *Gospel of Mark*, 230n71.

3. Culpepper, *Mark*, 385, writes, "The authorities were presumable investigating Jesus's disturbance of the temple activities on the previous day. Authority for direction of the temple lay in the hands of the chief priests. The authorities may therefore have been informally seeking to determine whether there were grounds for bringing Jesus to trial."

4. On the issue of "Jesus's authority was an issue throughout his ministry," see Culpepper, *Mark*, 385.

5. Culpepper, *Mark*, 410, is not so certain it is the Sanhedrin and refers to the sending party as "they," the same people in Mark 11:27 and 12:1.

6. See Köstenberger and Taylor, *Finals Days*, 39–42, for a good description of the interplay between Jesus and this conflict with the religious leaders.

ans—form an unlikely alliance. The Pharisees were loyal to Israel while the Herodians backed the rule of the Herods.[7] But Jesus was such a threat that two groups, separated by politics, join forces in hopes of defeating their shared "enemy." The Jewish group tries first to soften Jesus with flattery in hopes of tricking him into treason against Rome. Jesus is asked about taxes to Caesar and whether or not these taxes should be paid. A "yes" answer would allow the Pharisees information against Jesus that Messiah could not be disloyal to the nation of Israel and a "no" answer would allow the Herodians a chance to approach Rome and charge Jesus with treason against the empire. Jesus defeats their attempts to have him arrested (Matt 22:18–22; Mark 12:15–17; Luke 20:23–26). From Matt 22:18–22 Jesus responds with:

> "You hypocrites, why are you trying to trap me? 19 Show me the coin used for paying the tax." They brought him a denarius, 20 and he asked them, "Whose image is this? And whose inscription?"21 "Caesar's," they replied. Then he said to them, "So give back to Caesar what is Caesar's, and to God what is God's."22 When they heard this, they were amazed. So they left him and went away.

The Sadducees then take their turn, trying their best to make Jesus's ideas of the resurrection look unacceptable (Mark 12:18–27; Matt 22:23–33; Luke 20:27–40). The Sadducees were a smaller sect than the Pharisees but possessed great power, controlling the high priesthood, and were the dominant members of the Sanhedrin. Because the Pharisees and Herodians failed, they felt that they needed to step in as the party in power. Asking a tricky question based on the Jewish concept of Levirate marriage, where a brother will marry his sister-in-law if his brother dies, coupled with the resurrection: if someone has been married seven times but has had no children, when she dies, who will be her rightful husband? The Sadducees do not even acknowledge the resurrection as truth, Jesus retorts from the Torah (Exod 3:6–15). Sadducees only acknowledge the authority of the first five books of the Old Testament, Jesus knows this and defeats them on their own turf, responding with:

> 24 Jesus replied, "Are you not in error because you do not know the Scriptures or the power of God? 25 When the dead rise, they will neither marry nor be given in marriage; they will be like the angels in heaven. 26 Now about the dead rising—have you not

---

7. Culpepper, *Mark*, 412, writes that this combination is also important because "(1) the two groups plotted to kill Jesus earlier (3:6); (2) Jesus had warned the disciples to "beware of the leaven of the Pharisees and of the leaven of Herod" (8:15 RSV).

read in the Book of Moses, in the account of the burning bush, how God said to him, 'I am the God of Abraham, the God of Isaac, and the God of Jacob'? 27 He is not the God of the dead, but of the living. You are badly mistaken!"

After the Sadducees, a scribe (member of the Pharisees, Matt 22:34–35)[8] takes his turn (Mark 12:28–34). There are 613 commandments in the Law and this scribe tries to test Jesus's knowledge. Since many people did not own a copy of the Scriptures, people like this teacher of the law would be at an advantage. He asks Jesus which is the most important commandment. Jesus responds with the Shema from Deut 6:4 that what is most important is to love God with our all. Jesus then references Lev 19:18 attaching love of God with love of people (see Mark 12:28–34). This response would have impressed a teacher of the law knowing that most did not possess a personal copy of Scripture to study on their own. Jesus then denounces the scribes as a whole (Mark 12:38–44).[9] When people are threatened, their natural inclination is to try to eliminate the threat. The religious leaders first tried to discredit Jesus, trying to trick him into a wrong answer. The Lord was not discredited, answering in a way that affirmed his authority.

So broken are the leaders, their last resort is death. Having failed during the day to stop Jesus they must now plot to remove him by night. If Jesus can be killed, the peril of his being the Messiah would vanish. From Scripture, this was part of God's plan to fulfill all of the redemptive covenants of the Scriptures and to have Jesus resurrect from the dead, proving to the world he is indeed the Messiah, Savior, and Davidic King. From Mark 11:27 through Mark 12:40, Jesus is dealing with the religious leaders who should know he is the Messiah but are blinded by sin. Possessing no formal title, the Messiah defeats Judaism's best; this loss should have led the leaders to worship but instead, further escalated their desire to have Jesus removed.

After deflecting the onslaught from the Jewish leaders, Jesus takes his turn using parables to illustrate the leaders' spiritual blindness (Mark 12:38–40; Matt 23:1–39; Luke 20:45–47). Warning the followers against their deceit, Jesus uses strong words like "hypocrites" and "blind guides" while pronouncing seven "woes" in judgment. In the Gospels, Jesus is much harder on the religious leader than he is the person living in sin (e.g.,

---

8. Stein, *Mark*, 541, 558–59, is not so certain the motivation of this scribe is hostile in Mark's account.

9. See also Moloney, *Gospel of Mark*, 229.

John 4 and the woman at the well who had five husbands and was currently living with someone who was not her spouse).

On Tuesday, Jesus taught in parables, warning society about the danger of the current religious leaders, describing the coming destruction of the temple (Matt 24–25), and teaching that he will return a second time. After nearly two thousand years, his followers eagerly await his return as Davidic King, Jewish Messiah, and Savior of the world.

Questions for Group Discussion and Personal Refection

1. Has anyone ever said or done anything against you that was false; e.g., spread a bad rumor about you in school?
2. Have you ever felt threatened physically? Why is dealing with such feelings in your heart better than trying to change your circumstances?
3. Read Mark 11:27—12:37. How does Jesus deal with threatened people?
4. Which answer by Jesus against his opponents stands out most to you?
5. From the religious leaders, we learn that placing our security in our societal position can poison our soul toward pride; how can we prevent this from happening?

10

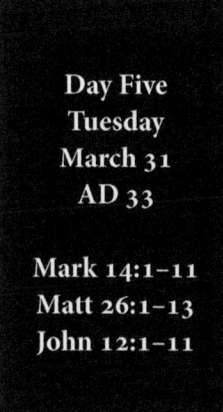

Day Five
Tuesday
March 31
AD 33

Mark 14:1–11
Matt 26:1–13
John 12:1–11

A Beautiful Devotion and a Devastating Disgrace

Before God can deliver us, we must first undeceive ourselves.

—AUGUSTINE

He must increase, but I must decrease.

—JOHN 3:30

LIFE'S JOURNEY DEEPENS WITH a self-sacrificing dedication. Personal pleasure is not primary. Chapter 1 of Rick Warren's *Purpose Driven Life* is titled "It All Starts with God," and the very first sentence, "It's not about you," epitomizes Scripture's life application.[1] Too often, humanity is concerned primarily for themselves: their personal appearance, feelings, happiness, and comfort. But the Bible is very clear, it is not about you, it is all about God.

Other than Passion Week, there is little that all four Gospels share, but all four possess an anointing scene.[2] J. K. Elliott states all four evangelists recording the anointing make it "on the same level as the miraculous feedings or the crucifixion."[3] Most scholars agree that the scenes in Mark 14:1–11; Matt 26:1–13; John 12:1–11 are the same event,[4] while Luke 7:36–50 is different.[5]

---

1. Warren, *Purpose Driven Life*, 17.

2. See appendix 1 for a more detailed discussion of the anointing scene in John compared with Mark.

3. Elliott, *Anointing of Jesus*, 105.

4. On the issue of the anointing scene as the same incidence, see Sabbe, *Anointing*, 2051–82, who suggests that John could be a redaction of the two Synoptic accounts; Elliott, *Anointing of Jesus*, 105–7; Van Til, *Three Anointings*, 73–82; Holst, *One Anointing of Jesus*, 435–46; Dodd, *Historical Tradition*, 162–73. Kurek-Chomycz, *Fragrance*, 346, notes the discussion of Luke 7:36–50 in Delobel, *L'onction par la pécheresse*, 415–75, as citing one source for the anointing accounts.

5. Keener, *Gospel of John*, 2:860; Legault, *Form-Critical Method*, 131–41; Bock, *Luke*,

From Matthew, Mark, and John, we see the emphasis of the gospel writers is Jesus's preparation for crucifixion and burial, with the application: devotion leads to death. In Jesus's case, he will give his life to save humanity (1 John 2:2) and in Mary's case, she will say no to worldly wealth and status in order to prepare her friend for the grave. Contrast their example with two other entities—the Jewish religious leaders and Judas—both possessing superior knowledge but unable to overcome personal inclinations.[6]

To test personal devotion, the first question that can be asked is: "What do I desire most?" Once this is determined, the follow-up question: "Is this something that can endure throughout eternity?" The final question one can ask is: "Who is the focus on?" These three questions can guide us away from immediate gratification into pure devotion and serve as a reminder that it is not about me.

The Jewish Religious Leaders in the Anointing Scene

The Jewish religious leaders could not accept Jesus as Messiah despite the obvious signs and wonders.[7] Already a significant presence during the previous days, they continued with their hardened hearts toward Jesus's messianic mantle. Blinded by pride, power, and wealth, while possessing superior knowledge of Holy Scripture, the leaders lost site of the kingdom of God. Instead of bowing down to worship Jesus as king, like the magi of Matthew 2, they plotted murder, volitionally preparing to break one of the Ten Commandments.

Since Sunday, Jesus has been in the temple teaching and performing miracles of healing. Matthew 21:14 specifically highlighted the blind and the lame being restored, a clear indication that Jesus was the awaited

---

690; France, *Gospel of Matthew*, 973; Nolland, *Commentary on the Gospel of Luke*, 352; Evans, *Mark 8:27—16:20*, 359; Witherington, *John's Wisdom*, 207; and Green and Hearon, *Anointing*, 13, who state that Mark and Matthew are one account, Luke is a separate one, and John is a "conflation of the two." Many lump Mark 14:3–9, Matt 26:1–16 and John 12:3–8 being the same story and Luke 7:36–50 being a separate account; cf. Coakley, *Anointing at Bethany*, 241–56.

6. France, *Gospel of Mark*, 547, writes, "Within this framework is a further sandwich which contrasts the hostility of the religious leaders and the treachery of one of Jesus's leading disciples with the extravagant love and loyalty of one of the least of his followers."

7. Usually listed as the chief priests, scribes, and elders (Mark 8:31), but France writes, "Mark does not find it necessary to produce the full list every time, and increasingly from v. 10 onward the avrcierei/j are made to stand for the whole group of opponents" (ibid., 549).

Messiah.[8] This is not the only place in Scripture where healing the blind and lame specifies Messiah; when John the Baptist was in prison and suffered doubt, Jesus dowsed his uncertainty by stating that "the blind see and the lame walk" (Matt 11:4–5; Luke 7:22). Isaiah's messianic references entail curing the blind and lame (Isa 29:18; 32:3; 35:5). Though it is obvious that Messiah has come, the very ones that should have recognized it most were the ones plotting to eliminate the chosen one.

Mary: A Beautiful Devotion

Sandwiched in between the religious leaders and Judas is Mary of Bethany, one of Jesus's closest friends,[9] who faithfully pours out perfume on Messiah to prepare him for burial. The anointing of her friend models pure devotion: forsaking personal pursuits for the glory of God. In anointing Jesus, Mary demonstrates that faith entails hearing the word of God and then orientating one's life around it. Jesus taught about his imminent death and resurrection (Mark 8:31; 9:31; 10:33–34), though the disciples had a hard time understanding (Mark 9:10; 32), Mary grasps what is coming. She knows her Lord and friend will face trials and hardship but also knows he will conquer death. Therefore, she takes very expensive perfume,[10] a costly fragrance extracted from the nard plant of Asia,[11] in an alabaster jar and anoints Jesus's head, body (Mark, Matthew) and feet (John).[12]

The gospel writers of Luke and John pay particular attention to Mary and Jesus's feet. In Luke 10:38–42, she is commended for sitting at Jesus's feet and listening to his teaching.[13] She next appears in John 11 after her brother Lazarus has died. In John 11:32 Mary met Jesus after his discus-

---

8. See also Matt 15:30–31 where the blind and lame form an inclusio over the two verses. The two begin the list in 15:30 and end it in 15:31 in an inverted manner.

9. In Matthew and Mark's anointing account the literary technique of intercalation is used. I will argue in an appendix to this chapter that John's writer is also using this technique. Mary is not named in Matthew and Mark's account but John states it was Mary who anointed.

10. The Greek word for pure/genuine has been disputed. See Carson, *Gospel according to John*, 428.

11. Many believe this plant is native to India or Nepal.

12. See Hendricksen, *Mark*, 558.

13. Green, *Luke*, 435, writes, "She is positioned 'at the Lord's feet,' signifying her submissiveness, particularly her status as a disciple (cf. Acts 22:3). The latter nuance is commended by her activity at his feet: she 'listened to his word.' For the Third Gospel, to listen to the word is to have joined the road of discipleship."

sion with her sister Martha, and immediately falls at his feet. The very next chapter—John 12—Mary anoints Jesus's feet with very expensive perfume and wipes his feet with her hair.[14] With so many references to Mary and Jesus's feet,[15] acts of submissiveness, servanthood, and loyalty espouse her faith. While the anointing of Jesus's head points to royalty,[16] the anointing of his feet communicates Mary's worship and submission.[17] Jesus is about to face his greatest challenge and fulfill the purpose of his life. Mary supports this by giving Jesus her best, continuing her example of how it is not about her and all about the Savior.

In terms of quantity, a pint is normally considered a minor amount, but in terms of aromatics, is quite large. Just a few sprays of perfume can fill a large room with its fragrance. A pint would make the odor in the room highly aromatic and powerful, sensed by all. This pint was not cheap; the value was more than 300 denarii or about one year's wage (Mark 14:5). Mark already draws out the immense value of this perfume by contrasting it to the feeding of the 5,000 in Mark 6:37; here, the disciples tell Jesus it would cost 200 denarii to nourish the multitudes.[18] The value of this perfume is greater than the cost of feeding the five thousand. To further illuminate the value, in 2014, the minimum wage was $7.25/hour. Multiplied by eight (based on an 8-hr. work day) for one day's pay, the laborer would earn $58 a day and $17,400 a year if multiplied by 300.[19] Imagine a bottle of perfume that cost $17,400 or more; this is what Mary poured on Jesus's head. The value is even more immense if one uses a household's standard income. In 2014, the US Census bureau reported that the US median household

---

14. First referenced in John 11:2: "It was Mary who anointed the Lord with ointment and wiped his feet with her hair."

15. In Luke 7:36–50, which most scholars agree is a different anointing scene, Jesus criticizes his host for not caring for his feet and his head while praising the woman who lived a sinful life for anointing and caring to his feet.

16. Elliott, *Anointing of Jesus*, 105–6, argues that in anointing the head this is a mark of Jesus's kingship. See also Beavis, *Mark*, 210.

17. See Robert Gordon Maccini, *Her Testimony Is True*, 176, in which he writes, "In anointing Jesus' feet, Mary is demoting herself from host to servant. . . . Mary's anointing of his feet shows her personal devotion and the subservient implications of discipleship. To some degree, Mary is an exemplar of how discipleship is practiced."

18. When factoring in women and children, the number would be closer to 20,000.

19. Whitacre, *John*, 300, writes, "Since a denarius was a day's pay for a day laborer . . . a rough equivalent would be something over $10,000, the gross pay for someone working at minimum wage for a year."

A Beautiful Devotion and a Devastating Disgrace

income was $51,939.[20] Either way, Mary's perfume was of enormous value. One way to show that "it is not about you" is to be generous with money and possessions.

When the perfume is poured, the disciples grumble (Matt 26:8-9). Almsgiving was heightened during Jewish holidays.[21] Familiar with its vast worth, scores of poor could have benefitted from its selling.[22] We know from John's account that the disciple whose criticism stood out was Judas (he will be discussed more below).

Jesus comes to Mary's defense as the ointment covers his body and feet stating that her action is a beautiful thing (John 12:7-8). Mary understands what lies ahead for Jesus and in faith responds by pouring the most expensive of perfumes on her Lord as an expression that he is about to save the world.[23] Jesus's disciples do not seem to fully grasp what is ahead until the events are over but Mary does: she believes and reorients her life accordingly.[24] She already demonstrated this in Luke 10:38-42 where she sat at Jesus's feet, now she will continue this belief by anointing her friend with the best.

Mary knows Jesus will die in four days.[25] Though the notion of losing her friend to death is disheartening, her faith is unwavering, keeping her heart afloat.[26] She remembers that her brother was dead for four days in a

---

20. See "Average Salaries for Americans—Median Salaries for Common Jobs," Fox Business, July 9, 2015 (http://www.foxbusiness.com/personal-finance/2015/07/09/average-salaries-for-americans-median-salaries-for-common-jobs).

21. Garland, *Mark*, 517, writes, "Caring for the poor was central in Judaism, and it was customary to remember the poor on holy days (Neh. 8:12; Est. 9:22). The complainers, as pious Jews, naturally think that giving something so valuable to care for the poor would be far better than pouring it down the drain; moreover, it would earn one a reward from God (Prov. 19:17; se Luke 14:14)."

22. See ibid.

23. See Hendricksen, *Mark*, 560-61.

24. Garland, *Mark*, 516, writes, "Some contend that this woman is the only follower of Jesus who understands the implications of his teaching. She knows that he is destined to die and seizes this last opportunity to express her love."

25. Moloney, *Gospel of Mark*, 279-80n15, believes Mary anointed Jesus on a Wednesday. The two days mentioned would constitute the evening of one day and the morning of the next. See appendix 2 for a more detailed discussion of the anointing in John compared to Mark in which I will argue that Mark's chronology of Tuesday evening is preferred to the apparent Saturday evening in John.

26. Garland, *Mark*, 517, writes, "According to Mark, Jesus is hurriedly buried by a stranger in a borrowed tomb, with no mention of any anointing of the corpse. This anointing before his death will have to suffice. The later attempt by other women to

sealed tomb. She remembers the overwhelming grief of her soul as she fell at Jesus's feet, then the joy as Jesus commanded Lazarus's rock to be removed, her brother wrapped in cloth, coming out of the tomb, and needing help to have his "grave clothes" detached (John 11:1-44). With one command, Mary's despair turned to joy; her darkness was overcome by sunshine.

In six days, Jesus himself will have his grave clothes removed. No one will command people to move the stone blocking the grave; the angels would have already done it. Mary knows Jesus has already assured her that his death will not be final; as an expression of her faith and devotion, she pours the most expensive perfume on her friend.[27] For Mary, money and position are no matter.[28] She has found the pearl of great price (Matt 13:46) of her life; everything else in the world has become faint.

Judas: Overcome by Greed

Judas is the saddest of all. A follower of Christ for over three years, he possessed a knowledge that only eleven others shared. Despite this knowledge, he could not overcome his greed and betrayed the one who loved him most,[29] for thirty pieces of silver (Matt 26:15), worth only about one-third the amount of Mary's nard.[30] He had heard Jesus teach, eaten with him, watched him perform miracles, witnessed resurrections like Lazarus, and had himself performed great works (Luke 10:1-12), yet in the end, his greed overcame him and he participated in a plot to kill his master for profit.

John makes note that Judas struggled with money (John 12:6). One would think Jesus would have put Matthew, the tax collector, in charge instead of Judas. Maybe Jesus felt Judas had a struggle in this area and allowed him charge of the money bag in hopes that Judas would reform his heart and crush his greed.[31]

---

anoint the body after Jesus's burial (16:1) is not realized because he receives a greater anointing from God."

27. See Moloney, *Gospel of Mark*, 280n21, on the breaking of the alabaster jar as a sign of unconditional devotion.

28. See Whitacre, *John*, 300, for a more detailed discussion of Mary wiping Jesus's feet with her hair.

29. Stein, *Mark*, 636-37, is not certain greed was at the heart of Judas's betrayal and discusses other potential motives for his betrayal; contra Whitacre, *John*, 301.

30. About 120 denarii.

31. Whitacre, *John*, 301, writes, "Judas used to steal from the common fund (v. 6). It is doubtful that this was known at the time, for if it was Judas would have been relieved

A Beautiful Devotion and a Devastating Disgrace

When the nard is poured, the disciple whose criticism stood out was Judas's. The waste of such a valuable asset probably miffed him. Since he helped himself to the disciples' money bag, having 300 denarii more meant Judas would have had more for the taking (John 12:4–6). The betrayer was more concerned about himself than others, which is why he stole. For Judas, it was not about God.

Contrasting Judas with Mary shows that responding to God's voice is not a function of quantity, for Judas heard God's voice every day for over three years, but a response of faith once the voice of God is heard. Mary heard Jesus and responded by pouring out more than 300 denarii worth of nard and being at his feet while Judas shunned God's voice and sold out his Lord for only one-third the value.[32] For Judas, it was not about Jesus or his colleagues in the disciple circle, it was all about him, and in the end, his greed led to his demise.

Despite the great sins of the Jewish religious leaders and Judas, God used their sin to save the world. Just as Joseph in Genesis was sold into slavery by his jealous brothers only to save the world from starvation (Gen 50:20) God the Father will allow his son to endure betrayal, false accusations, and unwarranted death on a cross for the redemption of the world (1 John 2:2).

Hebrews 3:7—4:13 gives a detailed warning not to harden one's heart when God speaks. The leaders and Judas did not respond to God's voice, but Mary did. God was able to use obedience and disobedience to bring salvation but in obedience, God's glory is experienced. To live in obedience means we must sit at Jesus's feet like Mary. Then we will be able to forsake the world for our glorious heavenly king and show people that it is not about us, it is all about God.

---

of his duties. . . . But such embezzlement reveals a heart in love with self and in love with money."

32. Whitacre, *John*, 301, writes, "Judas's heart is fundamentally different from the heart of Mary as she lavishes her love and respect upon Jesus. . . . We have the contrast between a true disciple, Mary, and one of the Twelve, which shows that privilege of position is no substitute for faith and obedience."

Questions for Discussion and Personal Reflection

What are some things you are ambitious for, either for yourself or your children or family?

1. Are these things that you will be able to be take to heaven?
2. What are some areas that you were once hardened toward but eventually heard and responded to the voice of God?
3. What is your favorite Scripture in the Bible? Why is it so special?
4. Why is money such a temptation for people to forsake Jesus?
5. Why do you think Mary was willing to pour out such expensive perfume on Jesus?
6. How is Mary's example applied today?
7. How can we remind ourselves "it is not about us?"

11

A Special Season of Rest

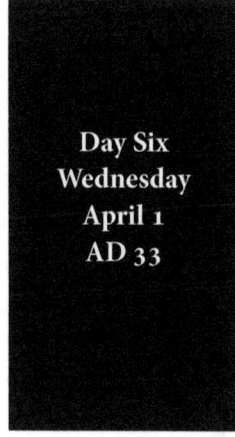

Day Six
Wednesday
April 1
AD 33

Sabbath is about withdrawal from the anxiety system of Pharaoh, the refusal to let one's life be defined by production and consumption and the endless pursuit of private well-being.

—WALTER BRUEGGEMANN

Let us, therefore, make every effort to enter that rest, so that no one will fall by following their example of disobedience.

—HEBREWS 4:11

LIFE'S JOURNEY CAN BE long, requiring seasons of relaxation. On Wednesday, five days after Jesus rested on the Sabbath, he experiences his second rest. The next time Sabbath comes, Jesus will be resting in a tomb. There is not much written in the Gospels about the Wednesday of Passion Week because it is likely a special day of rest.[1] The Jewish faith has at least twelve "special Sabbaths" that commemorate events or coincide with Jewish holidays. These are different from the typical sundown Friday to sundown Saturday rests observed by Judaism.[2] The one observed here is

---

1. Some scholars like Köstenberger and Taylor, *Final Days*, 47–49, think that Mark 14:1–2 happened on a Wednesday. Also, some view Mark 14:10–11; Matt 26:14–16; Luke 22:3–6 as occurring on Wednesday.

2. Rabbi Ari Kahn, a senior lecturer at Bar-Ilan University in Israel, writes,
   In order to understand the idea we must first explore the relationship between Shabbat and the other holidays. Shabbat and the Jewish holidays should be seen as different orbits. Shabbat is a commemoration to creation, while the holidays have an historical impetus. Moreover, Shabbat exists in a system established with, and as a result of, creation. Every 7th day is Shabbat, independent of any other calendric input. The Divine precept which introduced the Passover holiday began with a command to keep time, to anoint time.

(Taken from http://www.aish.com/tp/i/moha/48942426.html.)

likely Shabbat HaGadol,³ the Sabbath before Passover, also known as the Great Sabbath.⁴ The holiday commemorates the tenth day of Nissan, when the Hebrew slaves took the lambs that they were going to offer for Pesach and tied them up outside their homes, to keep until they offered it on the fourteenth (Exod 12:3–6). According to tradition, this was a dangerous thing to do, because Egyptians worshipped sheep,⁵ but, miraculously, instead of slaughtering the Hebrews, the Egyptians fought with each other over whether the Hebrews should be sent away.⁶

The book of Malachi is read in its entirety and a sermon is delivered in the afternoon hours.⁷ On this day, the lamb for the Passover meal is set aside. Rabbi Ronald H. Isaacs writes, "According to tradition, the 10th of Nisan in the year of the Exodus . . . was considered a great event, in fact a miracle, that the Israelites could on that day select for sacrifice without being molested by their Egyptian masters, who, at other times, would have stoned them for such daring (Code of Jewish Law, Orach Chayyim 430:1)."⁸

The details on Jesus's Wednesday activities are murky at best. Some scholars will advocate that Jesus continually taught in the temple, which probably occurred (Luke 21:37–38), and the Sanhedrin plotted to kill

---

3. According to Rabbi Ari Kahn, "The Shabbat prior to Passover is called Shabbat HaGadol. The source of the term is unclear as it is not found in the Tanakh or Talmudic literature, though in the Middle Ages a number of authorities occupied themselves with explaining the origin of the term." Taken from: http://www.aish.com/tp/i/moha/48942426.html.

4. See Tracey R. Rich, "Special Shabbatot," Judaism 101, *JewFAQ.org* (http://www.jewfaq.org/special.htm).

5. Some believe they worshipped rams.

6. See Rich, "Special Shabbatot."

7. The foundation of the holiday is in Mal 3:23: "Behold, I will send you Elijah the prophet before the coming of the great and awesome day of the Lord." Rabbi Ari Kahn writes, "The tradition, which accords Elijah a primary role in the Messianic age, calls upon us to read the portion of the prophet which alludes to that 'great' day." See http://www.aish.com/tp/i/moha/48942426.html. Also, from Judaism 101, "The special haftarah reading for this Shabbat is Mal 3:4–24. This messianic prophecy regarding the end of days and the return of the prophet Elijah is read at this time because it is believed that Elijah will return at Pesach. This is why we include a cup for him in our seder rituals." http://www.jewfaq.org/special.htm.

8. Isaacs, "Shabbat HaGadol."

Jesus (Matt 26:3–5)[9] but, by and large, the gospel writers are silent about Wednesday.[10] For the second time in the last six days, Jesus rests.

Rest is crucial to God. In Gen 2:2–3, God rested from his work of creation, establishing a model for humanity. Sabbath days rest the body and mind while allowing time for meditation, spiritual reflection, and personal relationships. As cited earlier, Dr. Brené Brown, in her book *The Gifts of Imperfection*: "If we want to live a wholehearted life, we have to become intentional about cultivating rest and play, and we must work to let go of exhaustion as a status symbol and productivity as self-worth."[11] The Jewish culture cultivates this by setting aside one day a week for rest as well as special times of rest throughout the year. During the final ten days of Jesus's role as Isaiah's Suffering Servant, the Messiah physically rested twice.[12]

Life's busyness often is fueled by humankind's need to matter. Action is associated with achievement. But during the most important time of Jesus's life—his last ten days as Suffering Servant—he took a break twice to physically rest. If Jesus can rest during the last days of his life, should not humanity follow his example?

Questions for Discussion and Personal Reflection

Do you have any special times of rest?

1. Is there anything you celebrate unique to your own life outside the cultural holidays?
2. Are there any spiritual milestones in your life that could be commemorated by a personal celebration?
3. How can these special times of celebration help us focus on God?
4. How does Jesus's example of resting while engaged in the most important part of his life an example on how to live ours?

---

9. Throughout Jesus's ministry, this was an issue and certainly would not be unique to a specific day or used as a day marker.

10. There are certain groups that hold to the positions that Jesus was crucified on a Tuesday or Wednesday. Wednesday would not be a possibility due to being a special Sabbath and Tuesday would not fit the chronology as the special Sabbath would be too early and not during Passover / Feast of Unleavened bread period.

11. Brown, *Gifts of Imperfection*, 102.

12. And a third time after the crucifixion.

12

Not the Last Supper

> Day Seven
> Thursday
> April 2
> AD 33
>
> Mark 14:12–26
> Matt 26:17–30
> Luke 22:7–23
> John 13:1–38ff.

You have not lived today until you have done something for someone who can never repay you.

—JOHN BUNYAN

But I am among you as the one who serves . . . and I assign to you . . . a kingdom, that you may eat and drink at my table.

—LUKE 22:27, 29–30

LIFE'S JOURNEY IS ENRICHED by service and hope. Thursday,[1] the seventh day, Jesus models and teaches about them. During the "Last Supper,"[2] references to foot washing describes Jesus's attending to his disciples, a model to his followers.[3] The feet would be some of the dirtiest parts of the body during Jesus's time having to trudge through dirt, mud, animal fecal matter, and refuse. Usually, a servant performed the duty of washing away such grime, but there was not a servant present to wipe the feet during the meal. Maybe the ones who were to perform this duty were celebrating themselves or maybe Jesus did not want his location known by too many people, or, most likely, Jesus made arrangements for a servant not to be present so he

---

1. In the Jewish mind, this meal actually takes place on Nisan 15 which would be considered Friday for the Jew. A day in Judaism is sundown to sundown and a new day begins once the sun sets in the evening.

2. It will be discussed later that Jesus himself did not see this as a last supper with his followers.

3. On the issue of the apparent chronological issues between the Synoptics and John see Stein, *Mark*, 640–44, and Carson, *Gospel according to John*, 455–58. John 18:28 states that the Jewish leaders did not want to be unclean so they could eat the Passover, which would not be consistent with the Synoptic account of Jesus having already eaten the Passover before he faces the Jewish authorities. But Passover and the Feast of Unleavened Bread were celebrated together, eight days total. There would have been more than one meal to be "clean" for during this eight-day celebration.

could perform this duty himself to model true leadership as servanthood. This was a duty no one would want to perform and may have been one of the lowest duties during Jesus's time, but this does not prevent the Lord and creator of the universe.[4]

How Maundy Is Thursday?

Maundy Thursday[5] is usually thought of in dour sad images: Judas's betrayal of Jesus,[6] the intense sorrows in Gethsemane, and Jesus's arrest. Its images evoke great contrition. Even the sound of the word Maundy echoes dissonance, but Maundy Thursday should not be thought of in this light, referring more to the washing of feet rather than words like: betrayal, sorrow, and arrest. In the upper room where Jesus would celebrate Passover, he washed his disciples' feet, including Judas's, despite his imminent betrayal.[7]

Before Jesus left for Gethsemane, he made a powerful pronouncement in Mark 14:24–25: "'This is my blood of the covenant, which is poured out for many. Truly I say to you, I will never again drink of the fruit of the vine until that day when I drink it new in the kingdom of God.'" Christ was about to leave his disciples but assures them he will come again. When partaking in the Eucharist (Lord's Supper), thinking of Christ's return should be paramount, for Christ's kingdom was inaugurated with his first coming and will be culminated in his second (Matt 26:29; Mark 14:29; Luke 22:29–30). The Eucharist becomes a celebration of coming hope, not just past remembrance; future anticipation accompanies historical reflection.

---

4. Whitacre, *John*, 327, points out the word love is used 31 times in John 13–17 while only occurring 6 times in John 1–12.

5. Scholars are divided on the issue of chronology of this meal. Some like Culpepper, *Mark*, 488–91, hold to the meal in the Synoptics being on Thursday while John's Gospel records it on Wednesday. But John's reference to "before the festival of Passover could communicate that they are "about to have" the celebration instead of the "day before." Also, Maundy Thursday is also referred to as: Holy Thursday, Great and Holy Thursday, Covenant Thursday, and Thursday of Mysteries in some traditions.

6. On the issue of Judas's betrayal, Matthew and Mark indicate Jesus makes a pronouncement of his betrayal before the meal while Luke records it happening afterward. Jesus could have made the declaration twice and the authors are recording different occurrences. Chronology was also not as significant in the ancient times and the authors could be using it to highlight a specific teaching.

7. There are some discrepancies in the accounts like John's emphasis on feet washing while not even mentioning the institution of the Lord's Supper. See Köstenberger and Taylor, *Final Days*, 57–58.

The Passover Meal

The Last Supper is a scene where Jesus celebrated the Passover with his disciples. An elaborate array of organized events encompassed the meal. One event is the drinking of the cups to remember various stages of the Passover feast.[8] There are four cups of wine that are drunk during the celebration, when Jesus makes this above pronouncement in Mark 14:24–25; he is likely referring to the third cup: the cup of redemption.[9] The third cup commemorated the shed blood of a lamb that redeemed Israel from Egyptian slavery and later, Jesus will voluntarily allow his enemies to shed his blood to redeem all of humankind to himself and be the final Passover lamb.[10]

Singing concludes the Passover meal. The final hymn Jesus would chant with his disciples (Mark 14:26; Matt 26:30) would be from Psalm 115–118, the second part of the Egyptian Hallel Psalms.[11] Deliverance is a theme throughout Psalm 118 and Jesus is about to deliver the world from the sin that separates them from God. Most hold to Psalm 118 referring to King David or a king like him who leads the nation to victory over its enemies. Jesus is the Davidic king who sits enthroned over Israel forever. Indeed, he will feast again in the new kingdom when he returns a second time in glory and honor to complete the prophetic visions in the Old and New Testaments about a future unblemished dwelling with God. An eternal bliss waits when the last king of Israel returns.

Jesus had his last Passover meal on earth before he would be slain for the sins of the world and fulfill the sacrificial system dating back to Moses, but Jesus's death on the cross will not be the culmination; God's redemptive covenant will be fulfilled at the next great feast, the Marriage Supper of the Lamb in Rev 19:9 when Christ returns a second time. So the Passover meal with his disciples in no way shape or form is the "Last Supper." Christ himself makes it clear he will dine with his disciples again (Mark 14:25; Matt 26:29; Luke 22:18).

---

8. See Culpepper, *Mark*, 491, for details of the Passover liturgy.

9. France, *Gospel of Mark*, 569, writes, "Mark simply does not spell out how Jesus's remembered words fitted into the normal structure of the meal."

10. See also Wilkins, *Matthew*, 836–37. On the issue of text criticism and Luke 22:19–21, see Hendricksen, *Luke*, 959, 968–69.

11. During Passover, Pss 113–14, would be sung before the second of the four cups was passed, after the fourth cup was filled, Pss 115–118 would be sung. On the issue of the unity of Pss 113–118, see Hayes, *Egyptian Hallel*, 145–56.

Not the Last Supper

The Last Supper (or institution of the Lord's Supper) where Jesus ate with his disciples celebrating Passover is recorded in the Synoptic Gospels and cited in Paul's letters (Mark 14:12-26; Matt 26:17-30; Luke 22:7-38; 1 Cor 11:23-26).[12] All four of the above accounts of the Lord's Supper share a reference to: bread and its breaking, a blessing theme, a mention of Jesus's words: "this is my body," partaking of the cup, and explanation of the blood in reference to biblical covenants. Both 1 Cor 11:23-26 and Luke 22:19 make mention of the need for continued celebration. All this was inaugurated on Thursday.

Final Thoughts

Maundy Thursday is often thought of in gloomy images like Judas's betrayal but should be thought of as hope for an eternal glorious banquet to come and an example to serve others. The Last Supper is anything but last; Jesus foretells his future feast in the kingdom of God when he returns (Mark 14:25; Matt 26:29; Luke 22:29-30), hope abounds, providing an example we can emulate in our lives; he showed his followers what service looks like by washing his disciples' feet and taught his followers he would again drink the cup with them when he returns.

---

12. John 13:1—17:26 is also believed to have been a record of the Last Supper but some believe it was a fellowship meal held before. But most likely this is a specific reference to the Passover festivities, which would last eight days, not putting it at odds with the Synoptics. John does not delve into the institution of the Lord's Supper.

Questions for Discussion and Personal Reflection

The feet during Jesus's time were usually the dirtiest parts of the body and washing the feet was reserved for servants and the lowly; Jesus performed this duty as a huge act of service. What are some jobs today that would be equivalent?

1. What are some ways we can "wash the feet" of our spouse, friends, family, coworkers, acquaintances, neighbors?
2. Do you think of Jesus's second coming when taking the Lord's Supper? Why is thinking of Christ's second coming crucial to partaking of the Lord's Supper?
3. What happens when someone has no hope?
4. Why is the hope of Christ's return critical in the life of a believer?

13

**Day Seven
Thursday
April 2 AD 33**

Mark 14:12–16,
27–31
Matt 26:17–19,
31–35
Luke 22:7–13,
34–37
John 13:1–3,
18–38

The Sovereign Savior

God is the Lord of human history and of the personal history of every member of His redeemed family.

—MARGARET CLARKSON

But our God is in the heavens; He does whatever He pleases.

—PSALM 115:3

LIFE HAS TROUBLE. JESUS made this point very clear to his disciples during the Passover meal, but in the midst of trouble, God is in control and has overcome the world (John 16:33).

The distress of the world takes many forms: failing health, an aging body, losing a loved one, sickness of friends and family, natural disasters, human evil, economic collapse, and betrayal by those who are close to us. Despite Jesus's promise of having overcome the world, great suffering and pain occurs.

The agony is so great that many cannot believe in the existence of God. In a highly chaotic world, the absence of a benevolent creator is a worldview that seems to make the most sense. Perhaps the most often asked question by an atheist is: "How can an all-powerful loving God allow so much pain and suffering?" Without adequate answers, the doubter continues in their unbelief of an intelligent designer.

Others turn away from their faith after not finding a satisfactory resolution to similar questions, but during Jesus's final ten days, we see that the loving all-powerful God himself experienced the trouble of this world despite being Lord over it.[1] Sovereignty did not produce immunity to pain

---

1. Garland, *Mark*, 524, writes, "A single theme runs through each scene [Mark 14:12–31]: Jesus's foreknowledge of events" (brackets mine).

and suffering; Jesus experienced it so deeply that he asked the Father if there could be another way. But in the dominion of God,[2] there was not, and Jesus freely obeyed by enduring crucifixion in order to quell the pain and suffering of this world. In Jesus, the person who had all power to end his personal suffering, instead chose to enter into it so the world could be saved. Since Jesus himself chose to endure suffering, we who suffer today can endure it through his authority.

Sovereignly Enduring

On Thursday, Jesus tells two of his disciples—Peter and John (Luke 22:8)—to help with preparations for the Passover,[3] which must be eaten in Jerusalem (Deut 16:5-6). That evening, he will have one last meal as Isaiah's suffering servant.[4] In less than twenty-four hours, he will be abandoned by his closest friends at the very time he needed their support the most, he will be betrayed by someone he poured his life into for over three years, will be falsely arrested in the dark of night, participate in unfair trials before Jewish and Roman courts, listen to many false testimonies against him, will be beaten and ridiculed by Roman guards, be disowned by a close friend who swore his allegiance to the end, be innocently crucified on a Roman cross in between two convicted criminals, will die and be buried in a tomb. Thursday and into Friday show that the God of the universe, who was in control, chose to experience the pain and suffering of this world to its fullest. Despite having the power to stop the cruelty, Jesus withstood it for the sake of the world. While experiencing excruciating pain and agony on a Roman cross, being deserted even by his Father, his acceptance of injustice will bring grace to humanity.

The Bible does not portray a world without hurt, quite the contrary. God originally created a perfectly blissful world, but humanity fell and the

---

2. On the issue of δεῖ in Mark 8:31 signaling a divine necessity reinforced by Jesus in Mark 14:21 see Stein, *Mark*, 401-2, 648-49, 655, and Garland, *Luke*, 852.

3. Garland, *Luke*, 849, writes,
   His precise knowledge of what they will find reinforces the theme that runs through the Last Supper: what has been foreordained by God is also foreknown by Jesus. Because his predictions regarding securing the room for their meal are fulfilled to the letter (22:8-13), the reader can trust that his other prophecies will also be fulfilled. Jesus is not being swept away by events but is in command and is accomplishing his divine mission.

4. For a good comparison of Mark vs. Matthew's accounts of the preparation for the meal by these disciples, see Nolland, *Gospel of Matthew*, 1061-63.

world was marred. From Genesis through Revelation, sin has caused this domain to be a place of distress. But even this cruelty brought on by sin cannot stop the sovereign God from his plans, being able to use evil for good. In Gen 50:20, Joseph declares to his brothers after being sold into slavery by them over twenty years ago: "You meant evil against me, but God meant it for good." Almost nineteen hundred years after Joseph's words, God will use the greatest evil against his son to offer the greatest grace the world can know.

The world is filled with pain but none of it is out of the grasp of the sovereign Lord. Unlike Rabbi Harold Kushner who concluded that God could not control the world he created,[5] and thus rejected God's sovereignty, the Bible asserts that God is in control despite what appears to be a world gone awry. During the final ten days, we see a sovereign God in human flesh submitting to his Father in order for the world to be saved from damnation. In the coming hours, Jesus will endure severe hurt and suffering despite living a perfect life. Though having the power to stop it all, he will humbly serve humanity by suffering to its fullest. God was certainly able to end the suffering, but, on the cross when his son cries out in anguish, the Father turns away and chooses to sacrifice his son instead of saving him.

Thursday Examples of Sovereignty

Before Jesus endures the cross on Friday, there is evidence of Jesus's sovereignty before the Passover meal. Much like the scene on the Sunday of the Jerusalem entry, where Jesus gives two of his disciples detailed instructions to find a colt in order to ride into the city, Jesus tells his disciples to go into the city and find a man carrying water.[6] The two disciples head to Jerusalem and everything their master had told them came true.[7] They found the man carrying water and began preparations for the evening meal.[8] Later, his sovereignty will be demonstrated by predicting Judas's betrayal (see also

---

5. See Kushner, *Bad Things, Good People*.

6. Usually women carried water jugs.

7. Stein, *Mark*, 647, writes, "This once again shows Jesus's mastery of the situation. He is in charge of what is taking place."

8. Köstenberger and Taylor, *Final Days*, 54, believes the man carrying the water jug was a prearranged signal for the disciples and that Jesus had previously made arrangements. Though this is possible, the scene mirrors Jesus's triumphal entry into Jerusalem where similar instructions, predications, and fulfillment occurred marking Jesus's sovereignty.

Zec 13:7).⁹ Despite knowing someone so close will do something so horrible, Jesus does not try to thwart Judas's plot knowing that Scripture must be fulfilled.

Not only will Judas betray him, Jesus's close friends will abandon him. Peter boldly asserts he will stay with Jesus until the end but Jesus tells Peter that he will deny his master before the rooster crows.¹⁰ In a few hours, Jesus's predication will come true and Peter will deny he ever knew the man he followed for over three years.¹¹ Then the sound of the rooster crowing will be heard and Jesus will turn to face Peter with a facial expression of someone who was deserted by a close friend, crushing this prominent disciple's heart.¹²

When reading the passages that describe the events of Thursday, one thing is certain, Jesus knows what is about to happen and is in control. The worst of the world's pain and suffering is about to fall on his shoulders but never does Jesus lift a finger to prevent it. He knew it was time to commence the plan of the Father; he knew he was going to leave the world he had roamed for over thirty years and return to heaven. He knew the devil entered into Judas to betray him, but he also knew that the Father had "put all things under his power and that he had come from God" (John 13:3). Rather than using his power to summon legions of angels or to stop the soldiers from arresting him, he rises from the Passover meal, takes off his outer clothes, wraps himself with a towel, pours water into a basin, and begins washing the dirt, fecal matter, and garbage off his disciples' feet (John 13:4ff.). This will be a precursor to Friday, for, in the hours ahead, he will have his clothes removed again and hang on a cross to remove the poison and corruption, not from humanity's feet, but from their hearts.

On Thursday Jesus demonstrated that despite the pain and suffering he was about to experience, he was in control and would allow the cruelest the world has to offer in order to save it. The worst evil imaginable was about to be turned around as the greatest act of love and redemption in human history. His sovereignty will be witnessed throughout the coming hours of his suffering.

---

9. See Nolland, *Gospel of Matthew*, 1059–60, 1089–90, on the thread of Zechariah references in the passion.

10. Mark uses *twice*, some early New Testament manuscripts do not record Jesus using the word twice in Mark.

11. Köstenberger and Taylor, *Final Days*, 86n33, writes, "The reference to the rooster crowing was an idiomatic way of describing the coming of dawn."

12. We will delve deeper in a later chapter.

Questions for Discussion and Personal Reflection

What has been the hardest thing that you have experienced?

1. How did God bring you through those crises?
2. Has there ever been a time when you wanted to give up? What kept you going?
3. Has anyone, or yourself, ever struggled with the question of how an all-powerful and loving God can allow so much suffering?
4. How can the sovereignty of God help us through these times?
5. How can Jesus's examples of enduring pain for the greater good of humanity help us deal with crises?
6. Jesus knew he would suffer and had the power to stop it but chose not to. What does this say about God's plan to change the world?

14

The Sorrowful Savior

Behind every trial and sorrow that He makes us shoulder, God has a reason.

—KHALED HOSSEINI

"Abba, Father," he said, "everything is possible for you. Take this cup from me. Yet not what I will, but what you will."

—MARK 14:36

**Days 7 and 8
Thursday and Friday
April 2–3
AD 33**

**Mark 14:32–42
Matt 26:36–46
Luke 22:39–46**

LIFE HAS TIMES OF overwhelming sorrow that often precede God's abundant blessing. The world is cruel; pain can afflict us at any time from many different places. Some can be experienced naturally while humankind's sinister tendencies can bring on others. In a world of death, dying, and suffering, no one is immune, not even Jesus the Incarnate Christ.

Seeing the Savior's Humanity through Sorrow

Mark portrays Jesus's emotions very clearly (e.g., 1:41; 3:5; 6:6, 34; 8:12). Other gospels show Christ's humanity through events as his frustration over his disciples' lack of faith (e.g., Matt 8:26), or his weeping over a close friend's death (John 11:35), but nothing helps us understand the humanity of Jesus more than watching him experience sorrow and suffering. He is about to experience affliction more deeply than ever. In the next sixteen hours or so, as stated in the last chapter, Jesus will endure the sorrow of a close friend betraying him for money, be physically beaten and taunted by guards, flogged with whips; another close friend will deny he even knew him; he will listen to many offer false testimony so that he can be convicted of a crime; he will be ridiculed and scorned by multitudes, crucified on a Roman cross as an innocent man; and, then have his Father turn away from him in his most desperate time of need before breathing his last breath. It is not a surprise that Jesus would ask his Father if there were another way (see Pss 42:5–11; 43:5).

Pleading through Prayer

Jesus led his followers to a garden on the Mount of Olives called Gethsemane.[1] He already was in Jerusalem celebrating Passover. The law stipulated that the Passover feast must be celebrated within the city limits of Jerusalem (Deut 16:1–7) so Jesus does not return to Bethany. God's plan was about to unfold for his suffering to begin.[2] With this type of anguish ahead, it is no surprise that Jesus would beseech his Father to remove it. In Gethsemane, Jesus will plead three times to his Father for another way, but the Father's answer is no and soon his son's mission will be accomplished.[3] But Jesus's request is not totally ignored; an angel is sent from heaven to strengthen him (Luke 22:43).[4] Jesus will not suffer alone, despite his disciples' sleeping; help comes from above. Through Jesus's sorrow, we have a glimpse into the human side of the incarnation.

Throughout history, Jesus has been misunderstood and the object of much heretical thinking. At the heart of the issue is the relationship of his humanity with his deity. The Bible teaches that the incarnate Christ is totally human and totally divine. Already, the human mind is unable to grasp such an idea, which defies mathematics. Since New Testament times, groups like the Gnostics denied the body of Christ which later spawned Docetism, who argued Jesus only appeared human leading to today where Jesus is portrayed as a political zealot or a man who had great influence. Jesus's humanity and deity have been hard to reconcile over the years.

Others, who believe Jesus was God, find it hard to accept his humanity as a viable example to follow. Many who struggle with sin point to his deity

---

1. On Gethsemane, France, *Gospel of Matthew*, 1003, writes,
    Its exact location on the Mount of Olives is not stated, but the traditional site on the western slope opposite the city would be suitable. Unlike Bethany, it was within the bounds of "greater Jerusalem" approved for Passover night, was easily accessible for Jesus and his group after a late Passover meal, and allowed Judas to bring the arresting party there quickly from the city.

2. On the issue of the word "cup" and suffering, see France, *Gospel of Matthew*, 1005 and n19, and Köstenberger and Taylor, *Final Days*, 92 and n38.

3. In Luke 22:44, the Greek word agōnia is the basis for the English word agony and is only used here in all the New Testament.

4. Some manuscripts of Luke do not mention the angel. For a good discussion, see Garland, *Luke*, 881–84.

as an excuse for why he is too hard to emulate: "I am not God," is often echoed from their mouths. Yet we see on day seven and into the early moments of day eight that Jesus, despite being God, experienced deep sorrow almost to the point of death. Before he will endure the suffering of the cross, Jesus begs his Father three times if there is another way (Matt 26:44; Mark 14:41),[5] making him appear more human than ever.

Many often wonder why an all-powerful and all-loving God would allow such a cruel world to continue. Through Jesus we see that God, who had the power to halt all the turmoil that was happening to him—instead of using his power to thwart the sorrow—entered into it. He knew that choosing not to endure the coming suffering would doom the world he loved so much. Obedience to the Father's plan was essential or humanity would be eliminated.

The sorrow in Gethsemane was so intense that Jesus's sweat resembled drops of blood (Luke 22:44).[6] It is not uncommon for the body to sweat profusely during times of stress and sorrow; there even exists a medical condition where the sweat is literally blood called hematidrosis. The hematological journal *Blood* describes hematidrosis as: "A rare phenomenon characterized by blood oozing from skin and mucosa. . . . The response to propranolol and association of stress with the bleeding episodes suggests the involvement of sympathetic nervous system activation in hematidrosis."[7]

Peter Singled Out

While Jesus is praying and stressfully sweating, Simon Peter is singled out from the other two disciples (Mark 14:37; Matt 26:40).[8] Perhaps he is singled out because he previously announced a few hours ago that he would go as far as giving his life for Jesus (Mark 14:31; Matt 26:35; Luke 22:31) and here, clearly, is not fulfilling his promise. In Jesus's greatest time of need, Peter defaults on his pledged support and falls asleep despite knowing Jesus is in peril. Peter is about to compound Jesus's sorrow when he denies that

---

5. On the issue of Gethsemane being a Markan addition to an already present Passion Narrative, see Beavis, *Mark*, 214, and Collins, *Mark*, 673–75.

6. Bock, *Luke*, 1761, argues that Jesus sweating blood was metaphorical but modern medicine supports that it could have been actual blood.

7. Mora and Lucas, *Hematidrosis*.

8. But in Luke's account, he does not single out Peter and does not contain Matthew's 3-phase prayer cycle.

he ever knew him (Luke 22:54–62; Matt 26:69–75; Mark 14:66–72; John 18:16–18, 25–27).[9]

Peter was not the only one who pledged his allegiance; Scripture says all the disciples followed (Matt 26:35). Now in Gethsemane, Jesus needed their pledge to come true and chose his three closest disciples to help him during his prayer time. But the evening is late and morning was nigh and the three disciples' hearts were filled with sorrow (Luke 22:45), leading them to sleep, unable to fulfill their vow that they would protect their master with their lives.

From Sorrow to Suffering

After the third time Jesus prayed to his Father, he knew the answer to his prayer was "no" and the only way to save humanity from sin was to be the Passover lamb. Three times Jesus asked and all three times he acknowledged the Father's will was more important than his (Matt 6:10; 26:39, 42, 44; Mark 14:36; Luke 22:42; Heb 5:7–10). When Jesus arose from his final prayer, he saw the torches held by the temple guards and Roman cohort coming to arrest him. He knew that great anguish awaited him starting with Judas's betrayal but in about fifteen hours, it will end and his mission will be accomplished. Sorrow is part of life but it will not be permanent; there will be a sunrise after the storm. But Jesus must first enter the storm.

---

9. We will delve deeper into Peter's failure in a coming chapter.

Questions for Discussion and Personal Reflection

Why is suffering often the instrument for character growth (read Rom 5:1–8)?

1. What does the scene of Jesus asking the Father for a different way tell us about prayer?
2. How honest are you with God in your prayer life?
3. Has there ever been a time where you have asked God for another way?
4. If so, was another way provided? How did it end up?
5. What does Jesus's sorrow teach us about our character?
6. Is there sorrow currently in your life? How can Jesus's example help us navigate through our present challenge?

15

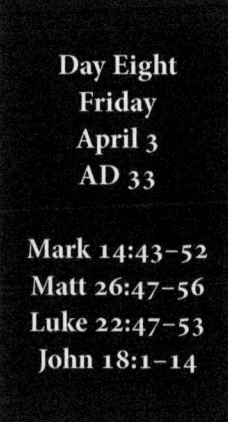

Day Eight
Friday
April 3
AD 33

Mark 14:43–52
Matt 26:47–56
Luke 22:47–53
John 18:1–14

The Submissive Savior

You cannot fulfill God's purposes for your life while focusing on your own plans.

—RICK WARREN

Shall I not drink the cup the Father has given me?

—JOHN 18:11

FOLLOWING GOD IS HARD. Many times it involves saying no to our own desires instead of taking a more desired path. Sometimes "no" must be said to things like a job promotion because too much time will be taken away from family and service; "no," to unethical business and academic practices because they compromise personal integrity; "no," to a personal or romantic relationship because our head is uncertain or unaccepting of the truth while our heart is confused with an irrational fear of aloneness; or "no," to our own desires for comfort and security, knowing that obedience to God would bring on distress. There are times where personal choices must submit to the Savior's plan despite more suffering than ease.

Some modern day ministers falsely ascribe following God as a way to enjoy health, wealth, and comfort, but, in the early morning hours of Friday, Jesus demonstrated that submitting to God's plan could bring the exact opposite. Knowing that great suffering was ahead, Jesus asked his Father three times if there were a different way, beseeching into the early morning hours.[1] There was not.

While in Gethsemane, Jesus knew that misery beyond understanding was ahead. In the end, his Father said no to his plea and Jesus obeyed, knowing he would experience incomprehensible pain and affliction. It will

---

1. Some hold to Jesus ending his prayer time on Thursday night instead of after midnight Friday morning.

start with his disciple Judas selling him out. The betrayer knew Jesus's location in Gethsemane (John 18:2), and led a large group of temple guards and Roman soldiers to seize his master (John 18:3).[2] He became the ultimate symbol of betrayal.

Gethsemane's Seizure and the Savior's Surrender

Jesus was in the garden praying. Judas arrived with the small army to arrest his master. Upon seeing the light from their torches and lanterns shining through the thick of the morning darkness and hearing the sounds of footsteps walking, Jesus yielded to his Father and accepted the horrors to come.

Judas's kiss is the first dagger through the heart.[3] He pronounces Jesus as rabbi, a term of honor and respect. The only other disciple in Mark's Gospel who referred to Jesus as *rabbi* was Peter.[4] The two disciples who disappointed Jesus the most are the ones who referred to him with the most honorable title.[5]

For only thirty pieces of silver—about one-third of a year's wages—Judas betrayed his master. Just a few days before, on Tuesday, Jesus's close friend—Mary of Bethany—had poured a highly valuable perfume over Jesus's head and feet worth a whole years' wages. Mary knew her friend was about to be sacrificed for the sins of the world and prepared him for burial. She could have used much cheaper perfume but chose to give her friend costly nard that was from a faraway land; Judas, for far less, chose otherwise.

Submission Despite Being Supreme

The large crowd of Romans and temple guards arrived with weapons in hand to arrest Jesus. During the next twelve to fourteen hours, Jesus will experience suffering beyond comprehension. The Lord asked the arresting

---

2. Whitacre, *John*, 425, writes, "The detachment of soldiers (speira) refers to a cohort, a group of 600 soldiers under a military tribune." But Burge, *John*, 491, states that a cohort is 1000 men (760 infantry, 240 cavalry).

3. Kernaghan, *Mark*, 305, writes, "When he (Judas) arrived on the scene, he went immediately to kiss Jesus and said, Rabbi! The breach of intimacy here is more disturbing... to betray Jesus and call him Rabbi at the same moment is tantamount to accusing Jesus of teaching him how to consummate a betrayal. It is as though Judas were saying, 'You taught me to do this.'"

4. Beavis, *Mark*, 216.

5. Ibid.

crowd a question: Am I leading a rebellion (Mark 14:48; Matt 26:55)? He had been teaching in the temple since Sunday, yet there had been no arrest, but because of the insecurity of the Jewish religious leaders, they chose the stealth of darkness, appearing more like criminals than the one they sought to arrest as one. The large size of the arresting group communicated that Jesus was a treacherous immoral, but if he was such, the Jewish religious leaders could and should have arrested him during the day. Jesus stated that the Scriptures had to be fulfilled (Mark 14:49) so he willingly submitted to the arrest,[6] despite already knowing what was coming (John 18:4), he chose not to deliver himself from the present danger.

Seeing the arresting group approach, Jesus engaged them by asking, "Who is it that you want?" (John 18:3–7). After hearing that they were seeking "Jesus the Nazarene," he replied by saying, "I am he," ἐγώ εἰμι or simply "I am."[7] All four Gospels in various places use the phrase ἐγώ εἰμι but none uses it more than John.[8] Almost twenty-five times in his Gospel ἐγώ εἰμι is used. No Gospel is clearer on Jesus's deity than John and his many uses of ἐγώ εἰμι would be a reference to Exod 3:14 where God tells Moses that "I am" has sent you. God wanted to be known and worshipped in Israel and would be expanded to include the entire world (John 3:16).

Jesus used this in John 8:58 and identified himself as God. The word Yahweh is "he is," or "he will be," Jesus stating that "I am he" or simply "I am," declared his deity, equal with God in Exod 3:14. Hence, upon hearing this declaration, the group in John 8:48–59 tried to stone him, and accused him of blasphemy.

Contrasting "I am" with the phrase "Jesus the Nazarene" encompasses a gamut from deity to despised. Reference to "I am," is calling oneself God, but to be called a Nazarene was to be loathed. Nazareth is not mentioned in the Old Testament and certainly was not a major city during Jesus's time. To be called a "Nazarene" was synonymous with being detested (John 1:46). So, within John 18, Jesus is referred to as both despised and deity but it is his claim to deity that displays his dominance.

---

6. See Kernaghan, *Mark*, 306–7, for a discussion on why Jesus stated that Scripture must be fulfilled.

7. See Köstenberger, *John*, 507n22, on the issue of the threefold repetition of the phrase.

8. See also Moloney, *John*, 485n5. Only John records the arresting crowd falling to the ground at the deity declaration.

Pronouncing Personal Divinity

When Jesus is asked if he is of Nazareth, he responds, "I am." At the sound of this declaration to the Roman and Jewish group, they all fall to the ground, revealing his power to deliver himself. When in the presence of deity, it is normal to fall to the ground in worship, but here, the people fall to the ground out of power. Jesus again declares, "I am he" (John 18:9), displaying supremacy to the temple guards and chief priests who want him killed. His power shows he could save himself but instead chose to submit to arrest. Jesus was never in danger and displayed his role as deity to the large arresting group.

By declaring deity followed by the crowd falling to the ground, Jesus saves his disciples. Those arresting Jesus may have not wanted witnesses and part of the large cohort may have also been to kill any observers to the crime.[9] With power that brings a group to the ground, they would not want to stir the pot by trying to kill others and focus all their energy on arresting Jesus. By displaying his power, Jesus shows he is in complete control of the setting and tells this large group possessing weapons to allow his followers to go free while submitting himself to arrest (John 18:8). Jesus will ultimately submit to crucifixion, allowing humanity to go free.

Seeing the arresting group fall down at Jesus's declaration, Peter is now emboldened; he takes out his sword and cuts off Malchus's ear (John 18:10).[10] Jesus declared this unruly and displayed his power again by healing the wounded man instead of trying to escape. His last miracle as Isaiah's Suffering Servant is to heal the very ear of someone who wished him harm. He could have summoned seventy-two thousand angels to fight for him (Matt 26:53–54) but submitted to incarceration while helping someone who was trying to hurt him.

Upon hearing this declaration and experiencing the power of deity, those arresting Jesus had ample opportunity to bow down and worship on their own, but, instead, they took Jesus away. Maybe the Roman centurion and those with him who declared Jesus the Son of God at the crucifixion were members of the arresting group and finally understood that Jesus was no criminal but the Savior (Matt 27:54). Perhaps they were friends

---

9. Mark 14:51–52 references a young man fleeing without his garment on. Many believe this person to be John Mark himself. See Collins, *Mark*, 688–93, for a good survey.

10. Moloney, *John*, 484, writes, "Peter fails to understand the significance of what lies ahead and draws a sword in a violent attempt to change the course of events . . . but he is rebuked as the passion must now begin."

of Malchus and saw Jesus heal their colleague in Gethsemane. There was something about Jesus that stood out; perhaps comprehension began in the garden when Jesus declared his deity by not using his authority and ability to destroy.

Jesus already declared that all of his disciples were safe in his high priestly prayer (John 17) here in the garden, his prayer continued and the eyewitnesses to this injustice of arresting an innocent man are spared. Because his disciples are able to run away, Jesus must face the trials alone.[11]

Submission brought upon Jesus great disapproval; his disciples deserted him, Peter would later deny him, and his Father would turn his face away while Jesus was experiencing catastrophic agony. By enduring this aloneness, Jesus could be with everyone. Submission often means saying no to oneself in obedience to God and Jesus submits to the Father's plans against his own. There may come a time in our own life where we will be faced with a similar situation, knowing obedience and submission will lead to suffering instead of security. From the Bible, it is clear that a greater experience waits if we choose God's way.

---

11. Jesus's trials occurred in six phases possessing religious and civil dimensions. Jesus had to stand trial before the Jews for three phases: (1) John 18:13–24; (2) Mark 14:53–65 (Matt 26:57–68; Luke 22:54); (3) Mark 15:1. The Roman dimension is found in: (1) Mark 15:1–5; (2) Luke 23:6–12; (3) Mark 15:6–15. Some hold to the first two trials of Jesus before the Jews as occurring late Thursday evening while the third phase occurred Friday morning.

Questions for Discussion and Personal Reflection

Why is it often hard to submit to God's plan?

1. Why is prayer such an important part of submission?
2. How is Jesus's submission an example to us?
3. What are things in our life that prevent us from submitting to God's plan?
4. What are the first steps we can take to help us submit to God?
5. What about Jesus's submission stands out most?
6. Has there ever been a time in your life where you failed to do what you knew God wanted?
7. What is the relationship between submitting to God's will and obeying God's word?

16

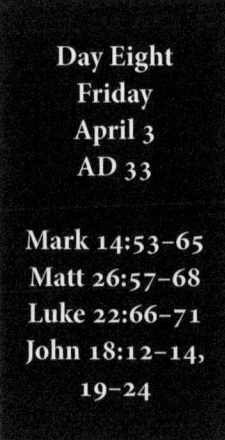

Day Eight
Friday
April 3
AD 33

Mark 14:53-65
Matt 26:57-68
Luke 22:66-71
John 18:12-14,
19-24

When Difficult People Assault

Unsafe people lie instead of tell the truth . . . only concerned about the "I" instead of "We," . . . condemn us instead of forgive us.

—HENRY CLOUD AND JOHN TOWNSEND

Answer not a fool according to his folly, lest you be like him yourself. Answer a fool according to his folly, lest he be wise in his own eyes.

—PROVERBS 26:4-5

THE JOURNEY OF LIFE will lead us to many. As mentioned earlier, some will bring us great joy while others will bring hurt. It is those who bring hurt that must be curtailed. Unfortunately, these hurtful individuals are unavoidable and must occupy a minimal amount of our time, emotions, and thoughts. To be around difficult people too much is a recipe for an unhappy life. They need our love, forgiveness, and prayers for salvation, but not our energy.

Throughout Jesus's life and the final ten days we have seen Jesus contend with difficult people, mainly the Jewish religious leaders. Day eight offered no respite. After being betrayed by Judas and denied by Peter, Jesus is face-to-face with the very persons who have wanted him removed since the very early moments of his ministry. These Jewish religious leaders were desperate to eradicate him. The longer he lived, the more of a following he would receive and reduce the influence of the leaders.

The Cowardice of Difficult People

These difficult people were weak, not having the courage to publicly arrest Jesus during the day, fearing his great popularity. Having taught in the temple since Sunday, Jesus could have been confronted by as many as six hundred to one thousand men sent to arrest him; they portrayed Jesus as a vile, treacherous, and dangerous criminal. In the darkness of the very early morning hours,[1] torches and lanterns were needed to find the location of the Savior. The Jewish religious leaders knew that if they made a move on Jesus during the day, the multitudes gathered in Jerusalem to celebrate Passover would turn on them and end their personal empires. Many of the Jewish religious leaders deluded themselves by thinking they were preserving and protecting Israel from Jesus, who, they felt, was a false messiah, but this delusion was fueled by Jesus's threat to their personal empires.

Throughout Jesus's ministry, the Jewish religious leaders saw their private domains crumbling, exposing their hypocrisy. The very people who possessed the most knowledge of Messiah were the very ones who wanted him dead. They could not separate their own agenda from that of God's. Being oppressed by the Roman government, the Jewish nation wanted King David to rule and return Israel as a dominant power, but Jesus came, not only as king, but also as Suffering Servant (Isa 53) whose focus was not political but spiritual, conquering sin and the authorities in the spiritual realm (Col 1:13–20; 2:15). The religious leaders could have repented for their faults but instead turned a blind eye to their hardened hearts.

The Arrest

Before the large cohort took Jesus into custody, he questioned his captors' motivation. Having taught in the temple during the day, there had been ample time and place to arrest Jesus if he were breaking the law. Furthermore, the blind were receiving sight and the lame were walking (Matt 21:14), the first two characteristics of Messiah prophesied in the Old Testament (Isa 29:18–21; 35:5–6). Even though the blind were seeing, the Jewish religious leaders could not. Instead of forsaking their wealth, position, and power, to align and support the Messiah, they could not let go and saw Jesus as a menace. When we feel threatened, our natural desire is to seek elimination of the object that is causing the threat. Some people will live in denial; others will create false circumstances. Some even will seek to remove the cause of their consternation through violence. When people attack, it is more a reflection of their own inner hurts than the person they are attacking and the Jewish religious leaders showed their hard stubborn hearts by seeking to remove Jesus in the darkness.

---

1. Though there are some who believe it is still Thursday evening.

When Difficult People Assault

Lying: The Way of Difficult People

Jesus was brought to trial.[2] The Jewish religious leaders tried to find evidence to convict but there was none (Mark 14:55).[3] So they had to resort to deceitfulness and break one of the Ten Commandments, not to bear false witness (Exod 20:16; Deut 5:20). When difficult people face reality, it is easier to go into denial than face the truth. For the religious leaders, they had to either acknowledge Jesus as Messiah or forsake their position as rulers and accept the end of their personal territory. They had to acknowledge that they were wrong, humbly proclaiming repentance before the people. But it was easier for them to fight for their position and deny they were ever wrong. In this case, they had to create a reality that Jesus was a criminal worthy of arrest. In order to do so, they lied.

False testimony was rampant that morning and people's stories did not match up. Jewish law required at least two witnesses to corroborate the charges (Deut 17:2–7) but none could be found. The penalty for false testimony was great; if found guilty, they would receive the same punishment as the accused (Deut 19:15–21). Despite this severe penalty for perjury, the religious leaders continued, knowing that their fate could be the same. It would not be crucifixion, for that is under Roman law, but death by stoning under Jewish law was certainly a possibility for fabrication, an offense of bearing false witness.

Finally, someone claimed that he heard Jesus say he would destroy the temple and build another in three days (Mark 14:58).[4] This scene never appears in John; only John 2:19 describes Jesus saying this, but we know that Jesus meant his body and not the literal temple. Difficult people will misuse what you say for their own agendas. When Jesus was asked about the validity of their statements, he said nothing; he knew they were trying to trap him and refused to engage in the foolishness.

The priests were in trouble and sought help. Knowing that Jesus considered himself the Messiah, the high priest, who himself was likely

---

2. On the issue of the historical debate of the Sanhedrin trial, see France, *Gospel of Matthew*, 1017.

3. Moloney, *Gospel of Mark*, 301, writes, "For Mark, the process is marked by false accusations and is a betrayal of justice from the start."

4. Moloney writes, "The Acts of the Apostles indicates that the relationship between the early church and the temple was important, but at times uneasy (Acts 2:46, 49; 3:1; 19:46; 24:53)" (ibid., 302).

growing impatient with the futile witnesses,[5] asked Jesus this question: "Are you the Christ, the Son of God?" (Matt 26:63). For the high priest to state the question in this mode, Jesus had a legal obligation to respond.[6] If he remained silent, then his enemies could trap him by saying he denied being Messiah and thereby brand him a liar while also being guilty of not answering. If he said yes, then they could again resort to false testimony in order to trap him.

Jesus not only answered yes but also said, "I am," claiming not just Messianic but a divine position (Mark 14:62),[7] then cited Dan 7:13 and Ps 110:1-2 referring himself as "the Son of Man seated at the right hand of Power, and coming with the clouds of heaven."[8] At this declaration, the high priest had only two options: bow down and worship or condemn Jesus as blasphemous.[9] He ripped his clothes and declared blasphemy then sentenced Jesus to death.[10] The high priest knew that witnesses were a waste of time and seized the moment to condemn his opponent.[11]

After his enemies whisked the falsely accused away, the true Messiah was beaten and mocked (Mark 14:65). The easiest way to feel better about oneself is to denigrate another; the guards beat, spat upon, and mocked Jesus for their own pleasure. In a matter of hours, Jesus would be nailed on a cross for them and the rest of humankind.

---

5. See also Köstenberger and Taylor, *Final Days*, 110.

6. Only John 18:13 records Jesus before Annas, the former high priest before Caiaphas. For a good summary of Annas, see Senior, *Passion of Jesus*, 58.

7. See also Moloney, *Gospel of Mark*, 304-5.

8. France, *Gospel of Matthew*, 1020-21, writes, "While a claim to be the Messiah was not in itself blasphemous, what Jesus said in response to the high priest went far beyond that claim: he was not only Messiah and Son of God but also, as the Son of Man predicted in Dan 7:13-14, he was now to share God's throne."

9. France writes, "Such outrageous claims must either be accepted, which was unthinkable, or repudiated as blasphemous and their author eliminated as a threat to orthodox religious belief" (ibid., 1021). But the high priest knew of Lazarus's resurrection (John 12:2-11) and the healing of the blind and lame in the temple (Matt 21:14) so Jesus's claims has recent evidence he is not just falsely attributing himself this glorified mantle.

10. Köstenberger and Taylor, *Final Days*, 110, write, "This affirmation seals Jesus's death. . . . Jesus has blasphemed by claiming to be the Son of God. . . . Politically, Jesus has claimed to be the one who will come as God's agent to receive cosmic kingship—this was unacceptable to the Romans who recognized only one emperor."

11. See also Moloney, *Gospel of Mark*, 306-7.

Roman Trials

The religious leaders had great authority but did not have the authority to pronounce a death sentence, only Rome could. Hence, Jesus had to stand trial before the Romans. In all this suffering, Jesus did not seek retaliation or vindication knowing thoroughly the Father's way. He could have easily saved himself from the leaders but chose to give his life so that they too, the ones who hated him, could someday have the chance to love him. On day eight, we see Jesus being assaulted by people whom he makes uncomfortable; instead of fighting back, he submitted himself to the Father's higher plan.

Questions for Reflection and Discussion

Why does the Bible command us to "love our enemies"?

1. Why is it so hard to love someone who is actively trying to harm you?
2. Describe a time in your life where you had a "difficult" person in your life?
3. How have we failed to love the difficult people whom we have encountered?
4. Has there been a time where someone lied against you?
5. Why do difficult people need to lie?
6. How can Jesus's example help us love difficult people?

17

Preparation for Greatness

Day Eight
Friday
April 3
AD 33

Mark 14:53-54, 66-72
Matt 26:58, 69-75
Luke 22:54-62
John 18:15-18, 25-27

It's fine to celebrate success but it is more important to heed the lessons of failure.

—BILL GATES

Failures are finger posts on the road to achievement.

—C.S. LEWIS

The Lord turned and looked straight at Peter. Then Peter remembered the word the Lord had spoken to him: "Before the rooster crows today, you will disown me three times." And he went outside and wept bitterly.

—LUKE 22:61-62

IN LIFE, WE WILL experience failure. Whether it is school, job, relationships, parenting, or service, failure can serve as a life buoy. The pain can be so great that some try to avoid it at all cost, but the pain of failure is almost unavoidable. Only those who never try will never fail, but failing to try stunts the very essence of life and can ruin the soul.

For most people, failure was frowned upon during their youth, and achievement was paramount. It was important to be successful in every endeavor. Whether it was academics, music, sports, or occupational, in order to have respect in the community, one needed to succeed; if failure ever occurred, it needed to be hidden. This created an unhealthy view of life and the fear of failure choked joy; if success was not achieved, shame would follow. The Bible teaches something very different: failure is not fatal but part of the preparation process.

Christianity in and of itself is a call to greatness. God is a great God and expects his followers to emulate him, but in order to become great, we must be broken, and failure is one of the means God uses. The greatness does not mean achievement, more focused on character development and obedience. In God's preparation for Peter to lead Christianity after Jesus's return to heaven, God allowed him to fail his master miserably.

Peter's Preparation for Greatness

The Apostle Peter is one of the church's great people, respected in all of Christendom. Catholicism reveres him as the first pope while Protestantism reveres him as the rock that built the church. But Peter was not always respectable; in fact, Scripture shows that before Peter became great, he wretchedly flopped.[1]

After Jesus was arrested, Peter and John followed from a distance.[2] John apparently had a relationship with the high priest and was able to usher himself and Peter into the courts. Jesus was led first to Annas (John 18:13), the former high priest, and then into the presence of Caiaphas, the current high priest and Annas's son-in-law.[3] While Jesus was being tried, Peter was outside by the fire (Mark 14:66). He may have heard the high priest scream blasphemy and rip his clothes and the commotion of Jesus being mocked and beaten.[4] Only Peter and John followed Jesus after his arrest; Scripture has no account of any of the other disciples staying close (John 18:15). Perhaps Peter was still fulfilling his promise and has means to rescue Jesus. Perhaps he hoped Jesus would be released and that he could bring his master home or to Bethany in order to receive medical attention. But Scripture indicates he was moving away from his promise to never leave Jesus. Whatever Peter's motives, for now, he and John had not totally abandoned their master.

The biblical narrative shifts and John is no longer highlighted; all attention is on Peter. A servant girl approaches him and begins to question

---

1. Much is made of Peter's cowardice; for a good discussion of Peter's courage, see Hendricksen, *Mark*, 616.

2. The actual identity of the disciple who accompanied Peter is unknown. Many have associated this other disciple with John since he is also considered "the disciple whom Jesus loved." See Michaels, *Gospel of John*, 897–98. Because John's writing is the only one who mentions the "other disciple," it is assumed that the other disciple was John.

3. The Synoptics have Peter denying Jesus in the courtyard of Caiaphas while John says Peter was in Annas' courtyard. It is possible since they are related that they lived together or Annas still had a strong presence since he was the previous high priest.

4. France, *Gospel of Matthew*, 1017, 1021, 1031–32, states that as Jesus is on trial, Peter himself is experiencing a parallel trial.

whether or not he was with Jesus and thereby guilty by association. Peter denied her statement.[5] The servant girl would be one of society's lowest individuals since she was a woman and a servant, but she did not look down upon herself and singled out Peter. The apostle had no reason to deny Jesus in front of her; he could stay silent and ignore her comments.[6] No one would really have taken her seriously and she has absolutely no authority to do anything to Peter. But Peter felt threatened and worried that if people did find out he was one of Jesus's disciples, he too would suffer a beating, mockery, prison, and possibly a death sentence. He responded by denying her accusations.

Peter not only denies he was with Jesus but the expression he used was suitable for a formal law court, not a courtyard; he is denying Jesus in a very strong way, unnecessary in responding to a servant girl. Feeling very uncomfortable, he tried to move away but she followed close by and saw Peter standing around trying to stay warm, and again called him out and asserted that he was with Jesus.[7] Peter denied he had any association with Jesus for the second time. Again, Peter went so far as to use an oath,[8] strongly claiming that he had no association with Jesus (Matt 26:72).

Hoping her accusations had passed, Peter continued to stand around in order to stay warm but, about an hour later, and for the third time, he was accused of being with Jesus. His Galilean accent gave him away as well as one of Malchus's relatives seemingly remembering him in Gethsemane (John 18:26). This time, Peter not only denied his involvement but also called down a curse and swears he did not know Jesus (Mark 14:71; Matt 26:71, 72). When the word or concept of "curse" is used in the Bible, a

---

5. See Whitacre, *John*, 434–35, on the issue of differences between the Synoptics and John on Peter's denial. It is highly unlikely that Peter denied Jesus more than three times; some suggest as many as six denials. Whitacre, *John*, 435, writes, "The foil Peter provides helps highlight Jesus's regal strength and authority, the hallmark of John's portrait of Jesus in his passion."

6. France, *Gospel of Mark*, 620, states that she would be socially insignificant based on the Greek word for female used in Mark 14:66.

7. The Gospels possess discrepancies on who the second accuser was. Mark states it was the same girl; Matthew states it was a different servant girl; Luke states it was another, likely a male, and John states it was a group of people and not one individual. John's statement that there was a group of people would include the same servant girl in Mark, a different servant girl in Matthew, and another figure in Luke.

8. Köstenberger and Taylor, *Final Days*, 116, write, "The oath emphasizes to those around that he certainly is not one of Jesus's disciples."

Preparation for Greatness

strong connotation of "condemning" can be inferred.[9] Peter, by bringing down curses, in essence was saying "I or Jesus should be damned" meaning that not only was Peter not one of Jesus's disciples but also that God's wrath should be invoked.[10]

While many believe Peter is calling curses on himself, there is evidence that he indeed is cursing Jesus, the ultimate form of denial. God was about to pour out his wrath in a matter of hours, but Jesus's first "damning" was from his disciple who swore he would not refuse him. The Bible says that Jesus became a curse to save us. The law states that dying on a tree is a curse. Even though Peter denied Jesus in the most vehement way, Jesus would become a curse to save Peter and the entire world. This would be the second time a disciple deceived Jesus.

While Peter was denying and cursing him, Jesus was brought out to face another trial. From the place of the high priest, he was taken to the courtyard where Peter was. Hearing the rooster crow, Jesus looks squarely into the eyes of Peter after his third denial, saying nothing. Peter stares back knowing he has failed his promise that he would stay with Jesus until the end, having cursed his master and denied he ever knew him. Peter could only run away from Jesus's presence; downtrodden and in despair, his only reaction was to weep bitterly (Luke 22:61–62). The only way he could have failed Jesus more was to betray him as had Judas.[11] All of the disciples failed Jesus during and after his arrest, but the two highlighted are Peter and Judas.[12] Both betrayed Jesus but we know Judas was overcome by his failure and chose to take matters into his own hands by committing suicide (Matt 27:5) while Peter, who most likely also contemplated a similar action, eventually chose to accept Jesus's forgiveness and was restored (John 21:15–23).[13]

Scripture and early church history such as Eusebius reveal that Peter's failure was not fatal. After the resurrection, Jesus reinstates Peter by asking

---

9. Köstenberger and Taylor, *Final Days*, 117, write, "Peter resorts to the most drastic affirmation of truth he can think of—he calls down a curse on himself and solemnly swears that he does not know Jesus Such an emphatic curse likely convinced some of the bystanders—it was a very serious matter to call down God's wrath upon oneself."

10. Most scholars consider Peter to be cursing himself but to curse Jesus would also be a quick way to get people to believe he was not with Jesus. France, *Gospel of Mark*, 622, believes Peter is cursing Jesus against the popular notion that Peter is cursing himself.

11. See France, *Gospel of Mark*, 619, for a comparison between the failures of Peter and Judas.

12. Who both are the only ones to address him in Mark as rabbi.

13. See also France, *Gospel of Matthew*, 1034.

him if he loves him three times and each time Peter's response is yes, then Jesus encourages him to watch over the flock (John 21:15–23). In the first ten chapters of the book of Acts, Peter is the main character; he also would contribute two letters in the New Testament. Church history records that Peter died by crucifixion and did not regard himself worthy to die the same way Jesus did and requested to be crucified upside down. Through Peter's greatest failure and Jesus's forgiveness, we see that Peter was being prepared for greatness.

We will all fail in life. It can destroy us as it did Judas or it can prepare us for God's purposes as it did Peter. On Friday, before Christ was crucified, his disciple, who swore he would not leave him, was the first to curse him. This colossal failure did not prevent Peter from becoming one of history's great figures but was used to break his soul and receive Christ's love and forgiveness. Peter was being prepared for greatness and was allowed to disappoint his master in order to someday testify for him with his life. His path involved great pain and failure. We have all failed, from Peter's example; we need to let God use it for our preparation instead of letting it hinder us from growth.

Questions for Reflection and Discussion

Can you put yourself in Peter's shoes? How do you think Peter felt after he fails?

1. Describe a time where you failed and it prevented you from growing.
2. Describe a time where your failure was later used for growth.
3. In John 21:15–23, Jesus reinstated Peter. Is there a time when you were exonerated after you failed someone?
4. How have your failures led you to growth?
5. Why is fear of failure so debilitating to the soul?
6. One of the most often commands in the Bible is "do not be afraid." Why do you think the Bible commands us so often not to be afraid?

18

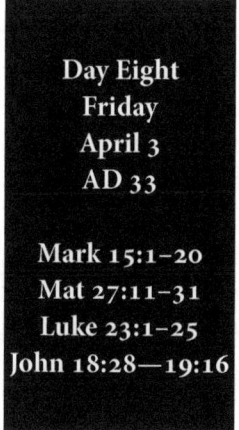

Day Eight
Friday
April 3
AD 33

Mark 15:1–20
Mat 27:11–31
Luke 23:1–25
John 18:28—19:16

Innocent Persecution

A man who was completely innocent, offered himself as a sacrifice for the good of others, including his enemies, and became the ransom of the world. It was a perfect act.

—MAHATMA GANDHI

For the joy set before him he endured the cross, scorning its shame, and sat down at the right hand of the throne of God.

—HEBREWS 12:2

JESUS'S LIFE EXPERIENCED AN indescribable torment beyond human comprehension. Completely innocent of any crime, yet leaders conspired to put him to death. Pilate knew Jesus was innocent and tried vigorously to free him (John 19:12), but in the end, the crowds swayed the Roman ruler. This did not deter God the Father's plan, who had designed to culminate redemption's plan set in place thousands of years before Jesus's birth (Gen 3:15).[1]

The Savior endured the Roman cross for the sins of humanity and now his followers are also called to bear the cross for the blessing of others. However, many of Christ's followers adhere to a different message, a false gospel. They have been led to believe that following God and obeying him will lead to health, wealth, and material abundance, not the abundance of the presence of God. On day eight, also known as Good Friday, obedience led to indescribable anguish. The Bible does teach that there is great joy and blessing within obedience; the book of Deuteronomy is very clear: obedience leads to blessing while disobedience leads to cursing (Deut 28). Nevertheless, the Bible emphasizes the spiritual dimension; the false gospel has transferred these promises to the material.

---

1. At least 2,500 years but most likely more.

Before Pilate

Very early in the morning, the Jewish leaders led Jesus[2] to Pilate (John 18:28).[3] The Sanhedrin did not have the jurisdiction to put someone to death (John 18:31). Had the Sanhedrin possessed this authority, Jesus would have been dead long before the cross. At first, the leaders just wanted Pilate to trust them and pronounce judgment without hearing any charges (John 18:30). Pilate did not oblige. They later came up with some offenses,[4] though Jesus was accused of blasphemy before the high priest, the Jewish leaders tried to acquire guilt of treason as a politically dangerous person (Luke 23:2).[5]

In order to receive a guilty verdict from Pilate, the leaders barraged the Roman governor with false accusations, trying to sway his opinion (Luke 23:1–2), but Pilate knew Jesus was not guilty of any crime against Rome.[6] Christ's ministry was three to three and half years accompanied by a growing fame. Roman officials would certainly have known of Jesus but clearly did not view him as a threat or else they would have silenced him themselves.

Pilate's first words to Jesus in all four Gospels are: "Are you the king of the Jews?" Jesus replies, "You have said so."[7] Moments before Jesus had to answer Pilate, Caiaphas asked Jesus a similar question: "Are you the Messiah, the Son of the Blessed One?" Jesus responded with "I am," a reference to deity from Exod 3:14 (Mark 14:61–62). This answer incensed the high priest, but not Pilate.

Worried that Jesus might be freed; the chief priests accused Jesus of many things (Mark 15:3). Pilate asked Jesus for a response to the indictments

---

2. Hendricksen, *Mark*, 628, believes Jesus was lead "to the fortress of Antonia at the northwest corner of the temple area."

3. For a good historical discussion on the person of Pilate, see Keener, *Gospel of John*, 1105–7.

4. Garland, *Luke*, 902, writes, "The Jewish leaders bring three precise and formal accusations that are political in nature and paint Jesus as a revolutionary firebrand. The reader knows that all three charges are patently false."

5. But later the religious leaders will appeal to Torah accusing Jesus of blasphemy (John 19:7).

6. Hendricksen, *Mark*, 628, writes that Pilate was someone who "exercised little common sense in handling the delicate problem of the strained relations between the Jews and their Roman conquerors. . . . It would almost seem as if he enjoyed annoying the Jews."

7. Garland, *Luke*, 903, writes, "Ancient readers in the Greco-Roman world would likely view Jesus's refusal to answer as a sign of his brave resistance."

INNOCENT PERSECUTION

but none was given, much to Pilate's astonishment (Mark 15:5).[8] The Roman governor knew the accused was innocent and also knew that it was for personal reasons that the Jewish religious leaders wanted Jesus killed (Mark 15:10). Perhaps, during Jesus's ministry, the leaders had complained to Pilate only to have him or other officials turn a deaf ear. The Roman governor was not fooled and knows Jesus was no threat to anyone. He had no formal education beyond the synagogue, no formal position, and only a circle of twelve, not numbers that would alarm Rome. The large crowds who heard Jesus speak posed no threat to the occupying Romans. Jesus clearly had a following but conducted himself in a manner where Rome was not threatened.

Christ did not respond to the religious leaders' accusations and remained silent, which means that Pilate must act, forcing the governor to make a decision.[9] Rather than dealing with it, he ships Jesus off to Herod, since Jesus was a Galilean.[10] Herod, who had beaded John the Baptist (Luke 9:9), pleaded with Jesus but again; Jesus says nothing and is sent back to Pilate (Luke 23:6–12). Now two officials have declared Jesus innocent putting the responsibility back into the hands of the Jewish religious leaders.

Dismayed that Herod's verdict did not free Jesus, Pilate had another way without subverting the desires of the crowd; it was the governor's custom to release a prisoner chosen by the Jews during Passover (Matt 27:15). Pilate offers two choices: one was Barabbas—an insurrectionist and murderer—or Jesus.[11] Pilate wanted the crowd to choose Jesus, knowing he was innocent; even his wife experienced an oppressive dream over Jesus's innocence and asked her husband to have nothing to do with him (Matt 27:19). Though Pilate had the power to free Jesus, he was overly influenced by the crowd's opinion; he hoped the crowd would acquit him of making a decision.

---

8. See Hendricksen, *Mark*, 632, on various reasons why Jesus would remain silent. He writes, "On four separate occasions during the last several hours of his life Jesus 'opened not his mouth': before Caiaphas (Mark 14:60, 61), before Pilate (Mark 15:4, 5), before Herod (Luke 23:9b), and again before Pilate (John 19:9b). These silences spoke louder than words. They were in reality condemnations of his tormentors. And they were proofs of his identity as the Messiah."

9. See Beavis, *Mark*, 225.

10. John's account of Jesus's trial is more complete than the Synoptics, see Whitacre, *John*, 435–36.

11. Barabbas's name means "son of the Father" and could be a contrast with Jesus being the son of God, see Beavis, *Mark*, 226.

The governor may have been familiar with the value Jews placed on life and how preservation of life was at or near the top of their priority list. Though uncertain if the term was used during Jesus's time, *pikuach nefesh* is a Jewish concept that stresses the importance of preserving human life as one of the highest virtues in Judaism. Those who are known murderers must be put to death because shedding of innocent blood corrupts the land (Num 35:31–33). Do not commit murder is one of the Ten Commandments, Pilate may have been aware of the Jewish views on human life and on those who have committed murder. In his mind, the crowds would surely put the murderer to death and release the innocent. Pilate was wrong as the crowds chose the insurrectionist.

Barabbas may have become an iconic figure in the eyes of the Jews, he unsuccessfully opposed the oppressive Roman government.[12] Some Jews might have thought of him as a hero but to Pilate, Barabbas would have been one of the lowest individuals, one he would gladly crucify. Roman citizens would have been murdered by Barabbas, and as an insurrectionist, he would have been a high priority for crucifixion and would have occupied the center cross that Jesus would in a few moments.

Maybe Pilate miscalculated the Jews' value of human life and did not think this man's "folk hero" status would override the fact that Barabbas had committed murder. Pilate knows the religious leaders were framing Jesus and was trying hard to save him. The religious leaders and the crowds were blinded. The law states not to bear a grudge (Lev 19:18) but the religious leaders could not let go of their disdain for Jesus and lead the mob into an irrational frenzy.

Pilate knew what they were up to and continued to harp on the sanctity, and proclaimed publicly that Jesus was innocent, not guilty of any crime against Rome (Matt 27:23–24). To crucify Jesus would be to commit murder, possibly the highest offense in Judaism and breaking one of the Ten Commandments. Pilate then washed his hands and declared he was innocent of Jesus's blood; the Jews, in an emotional rage, proclaimed that Jesus's blood was on their hands (Matt 27:24–25). In essence they said they were volitionally breaking the commandment "thou shall not kill."

---

12. Garland, *Luke*, 908, writes, "The rehearsal of Barabbas's crimes reinforces the miscarriage of justice against Jesus. By choosing an insurrectionist over Jesus, the hypocrisy behind the leaders' charges against him is exposed. . . . Barabbas is truly guilty of the very crimes they have charged Jesus with committing—inciting the people. He has actually sparked an insurrection, and worse, he has committed murder."

Innocent Persecution

Much discussion has taken place over how quickly the crowds could turn on Jesus. Six days earlier, the crowds cheered Jesus as he entered Jerusalem on a colt, but now, they were so angry that they were willing to commit murder, Pilate had already stated publicly there was no reason for Jesus to die (Luke 23:13–15, 22). It could have been a totally different crowd, one that had not been present on Sunday or it could have been a crowd who had expected King David to lead the nation against the oppressive Roman empire and were completely disappointed to see Rome crush this man in whom they had put their trust.[13] We know that Jesus came the first time as the Suffering Servant, which many did not understand. His second coming will be completely as the Davidic King but not just to free Israel; all humanity will be free. Clearly the crowd was influenced by the opinions of the Jewish religious leaders who were spewing venom against Jesus (Matt 27:20).

After publicly proclaiming innocence, Pilate then allowed guilt, currying favor by yielding to the demands of the crowd instead of what was legal and ethical. Perchance the Roman governor was worried the leaders would complain to the emperor that Pilate was soft on someone who was accused of treason but we know for sure that Pilate wanted to satisfy the mobs (Luke 23:23–24).[14]

Jesus was flogged by the governor's decree (John 19:1; Mark 15:15).[15] Perhaps Pilate hoped the crowds would relent; maybe he had hoped that the Roman flogging would kill Jesus and spare him the agony of crucifixion. It does not; much to the dismay of Pilate, Jesus must continue to suffer innocently and face a cross.

Pilate's soldiers then took Jesus away to his personal residence, the Praetorium, a place where soldiers gathered (Matt 27:27). Perhaps Pilate knew his soldiers would be cruel to Jesus and he will die from that abuse and not have to suffer the ignominy of the cross, and thereby preserve some form of justice, and free Pilate of personal responsibility. There were perhaps as many as 100–600 soldiers who mocked Jesus, plenty to end his life before the shame of crucifixion.[16]

The soldiers beat Jesus, mocked him, and put a crown of thorns on the Savior's head, but he did not die (Matt 27:27–31; Mark 15:16–20). Jesus predicted he would be beaten in Mark 10:34, so, even if Pilate wanted him

---

13. See Hendricksen, *Mark*, 638–39.
14. Ibid., 640.
15. See Carson, *Gospel according to John*, 597–98, for more detail on Roman floggings.
16. See Köstenberger and Taylor, *Final Days*, 146

dead, the Father already had a plan for his son to die on the cross. In just a little while, Jesus would die so those same guards could have eternal life. Even Barabbas, who had just been set free from crucifixion, would have the opportunity to be spiritually free along with all humanity.

After all this, Pilate again tried to free Jesus (John 19:4–16). He hoped that all the suffering Jesus had endured would be enough and that there was no need to take his life, but the crowds did not relent and rejected Jesus as their king by stating only Caesar was their king (John 19:15). Pilate appealed again to Jesus's innocence, hoping they would not commit murder while condemning a known murderer in Barabbas. The religious leaders could see that Pilate was trying to free Jesus and again shouted out for crucifixion. In a last ditch effort, the religious leaders appealed to their original declaration that Jesus had committed blasphemy (John 19:7), and threaten to tell Caesar that Pilate would not dispose of a traitor, which could have cost Pilate his job or even his life (John 19:12).

Pilate retreated back into the palace and brought Jesus with him. He emotionally told the Son of God that he had the power to free him but Jesus knew he did not; that power lay in the Father's hands (John 19:11). After hearing Jesus's words, Pilate again brought Jesus before the Jews and appealed to the fact that Jesus was indeed their king and that he will free him but the Jews reject Jesus much as Israel rejected God in the Old Testament by desiring a human king. They claimed there is no king to them but Caesar. Pilate gave up and handed Jesus over to be crucified.[17]

Jesus would make the journey to Golgotha and finish his Father's redemptive plan enacted thousands of years earlier. On day eight, we see that obedience led Jesus to incomprehensible suffering, but what waits is a joy beyond anything the world had to offer (Heb 12:2). To follow Jesus means to be hated by the world because the world first hated him (John 15:18), but through this hate, a pleasure beyond this world will be experienced.

---

17. Some have argued that John and the Synoptics are not in agreement in regards to time and day of Jesus's crucifixion. On the issue of John stating it was about noon and Mark 15:25 stating it was 9 a.m., or the "third hour," see Köstenberger and Taylor, *Final Days*, 142–43. On the issue of the Day of Preparation (John 19:31), John is likely referring to the preparation of the Sabbath during Passover times not the actual Passover.

Innocent Persecution

Questions for Personal Reflection and Group Discussion

Share a time where suffering brought you closer to Jesus.

1. Have you ever experienced suffering due to obedience?
2. Why is the false gospel of obedience leading to material prosperity so appealing?
3. How does Jesus's suffering help us deal with the world's injustices?
4. Read Rom 5:1–8. What stands out? How does Paul describe suffering?
5. Many Hollywood films about Jesus stress the horrors of the passion. Do such films as *King of Kings* or *The Passion of the Christ* make us more aware of the price paid for our salvation?

19

Supreme Love

Day Eight
Friday
April 3
AD 33

Mark 15:21–41
Matt 27:33–56
Luke 23:26–49
John 19:17–37

Life in abundance comes only through great love.
—ELBERT HUBBARD

Greater love has no one than this: to lay down one's life for one's friends.
—JOHN 15:13

LOVE SATISFIES. THE SOUL has an insatiable hole that craves to be filled. The first human yearning from birth is food. Growing up, children must believe they will have enough to eat or they will become obsessed over it, doing things like climbing underneath tables to eat what has fallen on the ground and overeating if presented with abundance. For children, from birth onward, this need must be met or else a fixation develops.

Once the need for food has been satisfied, emotional attachment is next. Just as young children seek out food for their bodies, they seek emotional attachment for their souls. If this goes unmet, development can be harmed. Whether it is through parents, grandparents, significant others, etc.—once the soul no longer obsesses over food, it will search for emotional attachment through relationships. Therefore, it is important that this need is met through mature trustworthy individuals or else great hurt will be experienced.

But the emotional well of the soul is very deep and can only be filled by God (John 4:13–14). Humanity seeks satisfaction from so many places—money, bad affiliations, possessions, position, prominence, and power—but, at the end of life, what most people desire is more time with those who deeply love them. It is one thing to search for this love and another thing to find it. On day eight, humanity received a supreme love, the greatest was about to commence: Jesus gave his life so humankind could receive eternal life and possess the only love that can fill the infinite soul hole. In dying on the cross, Jesus offered the world an eternal love relationship with him (1 John 2:2).

The most common criticism logged by atheists is: if God is all-powerful and all loving, how could he allow a world with so much suffering to exist. On day eight, atheists and those with questions received their answer: in supreme love, Jesus takes our place on the cross so we can avoid our justified destruction.[1] God had a plan immediately after humankind fell away (Gen 3:15) and now on day eight, his son would finish it. Jesus's death provided a legal acquittal from our sin but the fulfillment will occur at Jesus's second coming. For now, humankind still exists in a world, which God has spiritually redeemed but is still experiencing sin's effects.

Headed to the Cross

After being flogged and beaten by the Romans, though he was able to carry it a short distance,[2] Jesus was too weak to carry his cross all the way to Golgotha.[3] This heavy cross, that became the instrument Jesus used to carry the burden of humanity, was too heavy for him to lift. Simon the Cyrene was ordered to carry Jesus's cross (Luke 23:26) and served as an example to all who follow him about true discipleship.[4] He may have been unaware that this was no ordinary piece of wood but that the Son of Man would become a curse to remove the curse that prevents humanity from fully attaching to God (Gal 3:13).

Women followed Simon and Jesus to Golgotha, weeping, as they knew Jesus would die. However, Jesus was not focused on himself; after the Father rejected his request for another way in Gethsemane, Jesus had one focus: to endure the suffering for salvation, telling the women not to mourn for him but for their children and themselves (Luke 23:28). He knows that in less than forty years, the temple will be destroyed and Judea will be ravaged, making life there an unbearable nightmare.[5]

Climbing up the small hill of Golgotha, the two arrive at the spot where Jesus will be crucified (Luke 23:26, 33). The Cyrene will leave, either taking his place in the crowd or departing altogether, but Jesus stays. In

---

1. There is a theological thought named *annihilationism* where the soul ceases to exist once the body has passed. This sentence is not a statement backing this thought.

2. Stein, *Luke*, 585, writes, "The condemned man was to carry his own cross."

3. Edwards, *Gospel according to Mark*, 470, writes, "Jesus is brought to a place called Golgotha . . . meaning 'skull.' Luke, writing to a Greek audience, omits Golgotha, which is Aramaic."

4. See ibid.

5. See Stein, *Luke*, 586.

the morning, Jesus is nailed to the cross in public so that all those who had clamored for his crucifixion could witness.

The pain was so great that Jesus was offered a concoction of wine and myrrh to deaden the agony (Mark 15:23).[6] After suffering all Jesus had suffered the past sixteen hours or so, this offer would be tempting, but Jesus rejected the potion. He did not want his senses numb during the culmination of his mission. Over thirty-three years earlier, magi from the east offered up myrrh to Jesus as worship (Matt 2:11). The gift was accepted, but now, as Jesus fulfilled the plan and would die as king, the very king the magi traveled a far distance to adore, Jesus rejected the myrrh.[7] Moments from now, his body will be covered by it (John 19:39–40).

As Jesus was hanging from the cross, his charge was on display for all to see. Was it blasphemy declared by the high priest?[8] No, a sign above Jesus read "Jesus of Nazareth, the King of the Jews," a statement that Jesus was trying to lead a rebellion against Rome (John 19:19). The chief priests asked Pilate not to write this, but Pilate finally had had enough of currying favor to the religious leaders and told them that this sign would stand (John 19:21–22). It was written in Aramaic, for all the Jews to see; Latin, for all the Romans to see, and Greek, which was the language of commerce in the entire world. In essence, everyone would know that Jesus was the King of the Jews (John 19:20). People from all over the world would hear of this innocent person's death accompanied by stories of Christ's power, love, and teachings. Through this sign, many would have the chance to believe. Maybe Rome was trying to send a message to any other insurrectionists that if they tried to rebel and overthrow Rome, this would be their fate. Maybe Rome was trying to make a statement that they defeated Israel's supposed king. But, in the end, God used the sign to proclaim salvation through his son, the King of the Jews.

Jesus was nailed in between two thieves (John 19:18), but, most likely, they too, like Barabbas, were insurrectionists (Mark 15:27) and may have been part of the same band as the one acquitted in place of the Savior.[9] Per-

---

6. Edwards, *Gospel according to Mark*, 471, writes that this concoction, "an allusion to the suffering of the righteous man graphically described in Ps 69:21, was a primitive narcotic offered to deaden the pain of crucifixion victims."

7. See ibid.

8. Ibid., 473, writes, "*Blasphēmia* is used almost exclusively in both Greek and biblical literature of evil speech against God—making the chief priests and scribes guilty of the very thing Jesus was condemned for by the Sanhedrin."

9. See France, *Gospel of Mark*, 646, and Moloney, *Gospel of Mark*, 322n242.

haps Pilate wanted to ensure the emperor would not accuse him of being soft on a traitor; so he wrote King of the Jews over Jesus. Perhaps Pilate himself saw that there was something special in Jesus and declared to the world that Jesus indeed was a king. But, unlike the magi, instead of bowing down and worshipping, Pilate sentenced him to crucifixion.

Dying for Those Who Mock

The crowds that had demanded Jesus be crucified were mocking him as he hung between heaven and earth (Luke 23:35). The Jewish leaders who had incited the mob to crucify continued to barrage him as he was bleeding to death, unaware that Jesus was fulfilling hundreds of years of prophecy and is the sacrificial lamb of the world during the Passover celebration (Mark 15:31).

The two other criminals were also insulting Jesus, but eventually one turned as he watched Jesus's supreme love despite all the hostility.[10] The criminal saw Jesus not focusing on himself when being insulted but asking his Father to "forgive them for they do not know what they are doing (Luke 23:34)," a supreme love beyond human comprehension.[11] Despite all the insults hurled toward Jesus, the criminal sees a love that can only come from above. While the other criminal continues to fling abuse, undoubtedly due to his agony, the repentant criminal knows that Jesus is indeed God and asks for salvation: "Jesus, when you come into your kingdom, remember me." Jesus rewarded his faith and says, "Today you will be with me in paradise" (Luke 23:40–43). After Pilate and Herod proclaimed Jesus's innocence, the criminal hanging on the cross was the third person to acquit Jesus of any crime.[12]

What of Barabbas who should have been between the two thieves? The Bible does not record anything more. Perhaps Barabbas snuck into the crowd to watch the crucifixion and witnessed the supreme love himself. Barabbas knew Jesus was innocent; surely such an enemy of Rome would have been taunted and told he would be killed prior to the crowds' selection. Jesus was an innocent man. But Barabbas was freed and hopefully saw that he had a chance through true freedom by placing his faith in the one

---

10. Stein, *Luke*, 594, writes, "The supreme irony is that the criminal rightfully being executed for his crime(s) was infinitely better off than Israel's high priest, who by his rejection of God's Son was eternally damned."

11. See ibid., 589, on the issue of the prayer and textual criticism.

12. See ibid., 593.

who already took his place on the cross. Perhaps Roman soldiers followed him and killed him in secret or perhaps Barabbas ran for his life once he received freedom. But it is safe to say that no one in history experienced the opportunity for redemption like Barabbas. He had his life spared by Jesus's substitution and had a chance for his soul to be spared through Jesus's substitutionary atonement.

Three hours after Jesus was nailed to the cross, darkness fell over the land and persisted for another three hours until Jesus died (Mark 15:33–37). After six hours on the cross and enduring unimaginable suffering; Jesus could no longer hold it in. About sixteen hours earlier in Gethsemane, Jesus had asked if the Father could provide another way, but the Father said "no" and now, on Golgotha, Jesus voices another cry to his Father: "My God, my God, why has thou forsaken me?" (Mark 15:34). After his son had endured hours of suffering and abuse before the crucifixion and now experiencing the physical pain of hanging by nails on a cross for six hours, Jesus's Father had to remove himself from his son as all the sin of the world past, present, and future was placed on him.

This was the final straw; Jesus had endured the false accusations, desertion from his followers, betrayal by two of his closest friends, being moved back and forth to Jewish then Roman trials, being rejected by the crowds in favor of a murderer, being flogged by whips, beaten and taunted by Roman soldiers, and then being fastened to a the cross for six hours, but Jesus could not endure the pain of his Father turning away from him, But there was no other way. The sin of the world was now upon Jesus and the price of sin was death. Not until Jesus breathed his last could the Father look upon him again. In a few moments, all the hours of suffering would be over and Jesus's mission would be finished. His death was unjust, but, through the injustice, salvation for humanity was achieved.[13]

Mission Accomplished

Gasping for breath, Jesus could sense the end was near, what was once a cry of agony toward his Father now turned to a time of culmination. Jesus committed his spirit back toward heaven (Luke 23:46). The most excruciating pain of separation would soon end and the Savior will spiritually return to his Father's presence after over thirty-three years (Heb 9:24). With his

---

13. See Stein, *Luke*, 593.

last breath, Jesus stated, "It is finished," and the Old Testament plan was accomplished (John 19:30).

Upon Jesus's last breath, the curtain in the temple, which separated the holy place from the most holy place, was ripped in two (Matt 27:51). God told the world that no longer did a high priest need to enter the most holy place once a year on Yom Kippur; Jesus had entered heaven and finished this practice once and for all. No longer would animals need to be killed and blood drained; Jesus's blood had fulfilled the sacrificial plan of God and his wrath appeased (Heb 9:11–28).

Holy people who had died were raised to life and appeared to many (Matt 27:52–53).[14] This was a reminder that those who lived and died in faith prior to the crucifixion were not forgotten; now that Jesus had died, the sin had been paid for, and God's wrath had been satisfied. Their appearance placed another dagger into the hearts of the Jewish leaders, those the leaders revered became more evidence that Jesus was the Messiah (Matt 27:52–53). Not a criminal that they had tried to portray him as.

Not only did holy people rise from the dead, living people also converted. This was not the desired consequence the Jewish leaders had hoped in putting Jesus to death. The first to convert after Jesus's passing was a Roman centurion (Matt 27:54), a leader of one hundred Roman men. He was the fourth person after Pilate, Herod Antipas, and the criminal on the cross to proclaim Jesus's innocence.[15] Somehow, the way Jesus died showed him, much like one of the insurrectionists on the cross, that Jesus indeed was the Son of God.

His disciples had deserted him except John, but the women have not; they remained close to Jesus through it all (Matt 27:55–56). Jesus's mother, along with another Mary, the wife of Clopas and Jesus's aunt, Mary Magdalene, Mary the mother of James the younger and Joseph, and a woman named Salome remained near Jesus when most deserted in his greatest time of trial. They would know that Jesus predicted his death and told them he would rise, but the strain of watching someone so close to them endure such excruciating pain was emotionally unbearable.

The crowds who so vehemently demanded that Jesus be crucified and then hurled insults at him as he hung from the cross began to beat their

---

14. One of the most controversial sections in Scripture, see France, *Gospel of Matthew*, 1081–83.

15. See Stein, *Luke*, 597.

breasts, acknowledging that what they had done was wrong (Luke 23:48).[16] They had no idea that the person they were mocking was the very person who could give them everything they needed. As Jesus breathed his last breath in front of them, his spirit returned to the Father. Those who had yelled insults at him could later bow down and worship him as the true king and Savior (Rom 14:11).

Despite people's hatred, insults, and abuse toward, desiring nothing but Jesus's demise, the Savior gave his life so these people could be spared, the ultimate example of supreme love. "Greater love has no one than this: to lay down one's life for one's friends (John 15:13). It is a love beyond our comprehension, higher than the heavens are above the earth (Ps 103:11). Humanity thirsts for love, craving it to extremes, Jesus lived and died so we can have this love, a love that will quench our thirst (John 4:13–14). But in order to be satisfied, we must drink.

Questions for Personal Reflection and Group Discussion

We all need love. What are some ways you have felt most loved?

1. Think back to when you felt the presence of God most clearly. When was it? What did you feel during this experience?

2. Have you ever sought love in an unhealthy way? Why was it so unsatisfying?

3. Why is true love hard work? How is loving Jesus and experiencing his love hard at times?

4. How can we be more disciplined to think about Jesus suffering more? When was the last time you meditated on Jesus's suffering?

5. How can meditating on the cross and Jesus's death for you, your family, your friends, your enemies, etc., help you understand and experience God's love more?

---

16. Stein, *Luke*, 596, writes, "This involves not only a sadness over what happened but, due to the parallel in 18:13, remorse and the assumption of guilt."

20

Day Eight
Friday
April 3
AD 33

Mark 15:42–47
Matt 27:57–61
Luke 23:50–56
John 19:38–42

Good Friday through the Eyes of a Pharisee

For God so loved the world that he gave his only son that whoever believes in him will not perish but have eternal life.

—JOHN 3:16

NICODEMUS IS NOT MENTIONED too much in Scripture.[1] Only three passages—John 3:1–21; 7:45–52; 19:38–42—even reference his name. Despite

---

1. Because John's Gospel highlights Nicodemus over Joseph of Arimathea, this chapter will also favor Nicodemus but will also mention Joseph in a similar light. For more information on Nicodemus, see *Catholic Encyclopedia*, s.v. "Nicodemus" (J. F. Driscoll; www.newadvent.org).

 A prominent Jew of the time of Christ, mentioned only in the Fourth Gospel. The name is of Greek origin, but at that epoch such names were occasionally borrowed by the Jews, and according to Josephus (Ant. of the Jews, XIV, iii, 2) Nicodemus was the name of one of the ambassadors sent by Aristobulus to Pompey. A Hebrew form of the name (*Naqdimon*) is found in the Talmud. Nicodemus was a Pharisee, and in his capacity of sanhedrist, (John 7:50) was a leader of the Jews. Christ, in the interview when Nicodemus came to him by night, calls him a master in Israel. Judging from John 19:39, Nicodemus must have been a man of means, and it is probable that he wielded a certain influence in the Sanhedrin. Some writers conjecture from his question "How can a man be born when he is old?" that he was already advanced in years, but the words are too general to warrant such a conclusion. He appears in this interview as a learned and intelligent believer, but timid and not easily initiated into the mysteries of the new faith. He next appears (John 7:50–51) in the Sanhedrin offering a word in defense of the accused Galilean; and we may infer from this passage that he embraced the truth as soon as it was fully made known to him. He is mentioned finally in John 19:39, where he is shown cooperating with Joseph of Arimathea in the embalming and burial of Jesus. His name occurs later in some of the apocryphal writings, e.g., in the so-called "Acta Pilati," a heterogeneous document which in the sixteenth century was published under the title "Evangelium Nicodemi" (Gospel of Nicodemus). The time of his death is unknown. The Roman Martyrology commemorates the finding of his relics, together with those of Sts.

the paucity of biblical material, there is plenty to learn.[2] In these three passages, Nicodemus grew from seeker to secret disciple to servant.

In John 3:1–21, Nicodemus—a Pharisee and member of the Sanhedrin—approaches Jesus in the covering of the evening darkness. Being a member of the Sanhedrin, as well as a Pharisee, he would be well aware of both groups' plot to kill the Savior. Early in Jesus's ministry, the Pharisees and Herodians schemed (Mark 3:6), then the Sanhedrin followed (Mark 11:18). The entities join in their wishes to have Jesus removed (Mark 12:13). If the masses followed Jesus, they would no longer be aligned with

---

Stephen, Gamaliel, and Abibo, on 3 August.

2. One could interchange Nicodemus with Joseph of Arimathea. At times in this chapter, they will be used together as examples because their paths are so similar. Though Joseph was a member of the Sanhedrin, it is likely he was not a Pharisee, which is why Nicodemus will receive slightly more distinction in this section. A good summary on Joseph is found in the *Catholic Encyclopedia*, s.v. "Joseph of Arimathea" (F. Gigot; www.newadvent.org).

He was born at Arimathea—hence his surname—"a city of Judea" (Luke 23:51), which is very likely identical with Ramatha, the birthplace of the Prophet Samuel, although several scholars prefer to identify it with the town of Ramleh. He was a wealthy Israelite (Matt 27:57), "a good and a just man" (Luke 23:50), "who was also himself looking for the kingdom of God" (Mark 15:43). He is also called by St. Mark and by St. Luke a *bouleutes*, literally, "a senator," whereby is meant a member of the Sanhedrin or supreme council of the Jews. He was a disciple of Jesus, probably ever since Christ's first preaching in Judea (John 2:23), but he did not declare himself as such "for fear of the Jews" (John 19:38). On account of this secret allegiance to Jesus, he did not consent to His condemnation by the Sanhedrin (Luke 23:51), and was most likely absent from the meeting which sentenced Jesus to death (cf. Mark 14:64).

The crucifixion of the Master quickened Joseph's faith and love, and suggested to him that he should provide for Christ's burial before the Sabbath began. Unmindful therefore of all personal danger, a danger which was indeed considerable under the circumstances, he boldly requested from Pilate the body of Jesus, and was successful in his request (Mark 15:43–45). Once in possession of this sacred treasure, he—together with Nicodemus, whom his courage had likewise emboldened, and who brought abundant spices—wrapped up Christ's body in fine linen and grave bands, laid it in his own tomb, new and yet unused, and hewn out of a rock in a neighboring garden, and withdrew after rolling a great stone to the opening of the sepulchre (Matt 27:59, 60; Mark 15:46; Luke 23:53; John 19:38–42). Thus was fulfilled Isaiah's prediction that the grave of the Messiahs would be with a rich man (Isa 53:9). The Greek Church celebrates the feast of Joseph of Arimathea on 31 July, and the Roman Church on 17 March. The additional details which are found concerning him in the apocryphal "Acta Pilati" are unworthy of credence. Likewise, fabulous is the legend which tells of his coming to Gaul AD 63, and thence to Great Britain, where he is supposed to have founded the earliest Christian oratory at Glastonbury. Finally, the story of the translation of the body of Joseph of Arimathea from Jerusalem to Moyenmonstre (Diocese of Toul) originated late and is unreliable.

the leaders. The pride in their heart caused them to love the praise of people more than God (John 12:43).

Nicodemus was aware of his colleagues' desires to eradicate Jesus from the scene. However, being a teacher of Israel, he saw something that moved him toward faith in the promised Messiah.[3] Christ is not on earth just to deliver Israel from the Roman superpower but all peoples—past, present, and future—from the superpower of evil.

The most famous verse in the Bible, John 3:16, is in the context of the discussion the Pharisee has with the Savior. Jesus says to Nicodemus that he must be born again; the Holy Spirit must wash away the stain of sin and make him into a new creation. After Jesus explained to the Pharisee the need for rebirth, John penned this renowned verse: "For God so loved the world that he gave his only son that whoever believes in him will not perish but have eternal life." Nicodemus likely walked away from Jesus with eternal life, ceasing to be a seeker.[4]

Nicodemus next appears in John 7:45–52 when the Sanhedrin criticizes the temple guards for not arresting Jesus. He speaks up to defend the Savior but is silenced immediately. The Sanhedrin, who accused people of not knowing the law, freely disobeyed the law themselves when confronted by Nicodemus. Blinded by their pride, the Sanhedrin retorted that there had never been a prophet from Galilee. They should have remembered that Jonah (2 Kgs 14:25), Nahum (Nah 1:1),[5] and possibly Elijah had prophetic associations with Galilee, so Jesus would not be out of the ordinary.[6] Nicodemus could have remained silent when the Savior was being accused but chose to speak up in the Lord's defense. When Jesus is being attacked, are we silent?

Nicodemus appeared[7] a third and final time in John 19 after the crucifixion. Christ died around 3:00 p.m. Another Sanhedrin member, Joseph

---

3. This chapter takes a favorable view of Nicodemus's faith, for another viewpoint, see Vande Vrede, *Nicodemus and John the Baptist*, 715–26.

4. Michaels, *Gospel of John*, 177, writes, "Nicodemus 'came to him.' . . . Wherever this expression occurs in the Gospel, it raises at least a possibility that the person 'coming' in faith, or giving allegiance in some way. . . . This appears to be the case here."

5. Jonah was from Gath-Hepher, Nazareth would later form and only be a few miles away. Nahum was from Elkosh, a small village on the sea of Galilee. The well-known biblical city Capernaum means city of Nahum.

6. Most commentators acknowledge Jonah as being from Galilee. The other two are not as clear though good evidence points to them also possessing Galilee roots.

7. Along with Joseph of Arimathea. For additional information, see Keener, *Gospel*

of Arimathea, asked permission to care for Jesus's body and Pilate granted his wish. Though Joseph was described as a "secret disciple of Jesus" (John 19:38), it can be assumed both he and Nicodemus were "secret" disciples, not wanting to risk their standing in the Sanhedrin.[8] However, their effort to care for Jesus's body reveals they had given up their secrecy and risked their position to prepare Jesus's body for burial. For years, Jesus had threatened their colleagues; the enemies of Jesus have been hoping and waiting for this moment to eliminate him. At great risk, caring for a hated enemy could have led to personal disaster. The leader of the Sanhedrin could have believed that "the friend of my enemy is also my enemy." Another possibility is the Sanhedrin desired Joseph to have Jesus in his tomb so they would know the bodies whereabouts until after three days. Then they could dispose the body without fear of a fulfilled prophecy. Nicodemus and Joseph were likely aware of each other's faith given the fact that they both participate together in caring for the dead body of Jesus.

Nicodemus brought a large amount of spices and perfumes, about seventy-five to one hundred pounds in weight. He had in mind a "royal burial."[9] Four days earlier, Mary had anointed Jesus's head and feet with a pint of expensive perfume whose fragrance filled the room; now another seventy-five to one hundred pounds[10] of spices and fragrance would be applied, a burial fit for a king.[11] As the magi offered myrrh to Jesus almost thirty-three years earlier, now, Nicodemus will honor Jesus with myrrh as the revered king the magi worshipped. Myrrh is part of the beginning and the end of a remarkable life.

Both Nicodemus and Joseph of Arimathea would know that touching a dead body would render them unclean and disqualify them from further participation in the Passover festival. They would have to wait a month to celebrate (Num 9:11–13). As members of the Sanhedrin, the highest court in Judaism, their uncleanness during the Passover feast would bring shame and disgrace. Caring for Jesus in such a royal manner would also be an indignity

---

of John, 1158–61.

8. Keener, *Gospel of John*, 1162, writes, "Yet both Joseph, here said to be a 'secret' disciple of Jesus (19:38), and Nicodemus, who came 'by night' (19:39), now render a service to Jesus that is potentially dangerous—a service the long-term disciples were unwilling to offer."

9. See Michaels, *Gospel of John*, 982.

10. Some writers believe it could be as much as one hundred pounds of spices and myrrh. See also Keener, *Gospel of John*, 1163–64.

11. See Michaels, *Gospel of John*, 982.

to the other Sanhedrin members who had worked so hard to have Jesus convicted of treason. Wrath and punishment would clearly rain down.[12]

When Nicodemus was a seeker, he came to Jesus in the cover of the evening darkness, but now, Nicodemus came to Jesus in broad daylight. He could have hired Gentiles to care for the body and certainly should not have used such a vast amount of spices on the corpse but Nicodemus has moved to a different level of faith. In the light of day, touching a dead body and applying a large amount of spices to prepare a convicted person for burial, Nicodemus no longer is concerned about his secret. In his mind, the Passover feast has already been fulfilled in Jesus. Temple worship and sacrifice would cease because Jesus's sacrifice meant there was no more need to shed the blood of animals. Nicodemus was a good picture of the old covenant fading and the new covenant taking over.

Time was a major factor; it was almost time for the Sabbath to begin, so they had to hurry before sundown at 6:00 p.m. Other than John, none of the other disciples was in close physical proximity to the cross. Nicodemus demonstrated great courage to associate himself with Jesus while those who were his followers would not. At great peril, Nicodemus risks everything—great wealth, high status, power, authority, and membership in the Sanhedrin—to care for the body of the Messiah and Savior. He turned his back on his prominence as a Pharisee and disowned his position, as Paul did (Phil 3:1–12), to gain Christ. On this Good Friday, have we moved from "secret" disciple to servant? Have we sold and renounced all our worldly treasures to gain the greatest jewel? On Good Friday, Nicodemus became more than a secret disciple but one who would give up his life of wealth, power, position, and status so he could care for the lifeless body of the Messiah and Savior of the world. If Nicodemus was willing to give up his life to gain Jesus, are we willing to follow his example?

---

12. Many believe that the dead bodies after crucifixion were taken by loved ones or left to be eaten by wild animals. It is clear that the Jewish leaders know that Jesus's body is laid in a tomb. Whether or not initially they know it is of Joseph of Arimathea is uncertain but Pilate knew and could have informed them when they visited.

Questions for Personal Reflection and Group Discussion

What would a "secret disciple" be?

1. Read the story of Naaman in 2 Kings 5. Is his "secrecy" similar to Nicodemus's?
2. Why is it that one cannot remain a secret disciple forever?
3. Is it ever necessary, for a time, to be a secret disciple?
4. Nicodemus and Joseph clearly came out of their secrecy by caring for Jesus's body. Would most people be surprised if they knew of your faith?
5. What do you think caused Nicodemus and Joseph to take such a bold step of faith?
6. Was there ever a time in your life where you did such a bold action that clearly showed people you were a follower of Jesus?
7. Was there ever a time where you had to give up "worldly" prestige for the glory of God?
8. Can you see any decisions in the future that would challenge you to make a Nicodemus/Joseph type statement at great risk?
9. How does our willingness to risk our worldly standing demonstrate our heart for heavenly standing?

21

Breaking the Sabbath for Personal Security

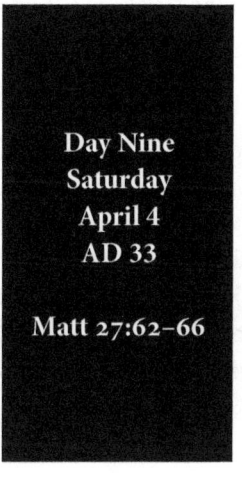

Day Nine
Saturday
April 4
AD 33

Matt 27:62–66

There will always be someone willing to hurt you, put you down, gossip about you, belittle your accomplishments and judge your soul. It is a fact that we all must face. However, if you realize that God . . . stands beside you when others cast stones you will never be afraid, never feel worthless and never feel alone.

—SHANNON L. ALDER

Jesus was not entrusting himself to them, for He knew all people.

—JOHN 2:24

SATURDAY SHOULD HAVE BEEN a Sabbath for the Jewish nation; no work was to be done until sundown. It is still one of the most important aspects of Judaism. In Israel today, it would not be uncommon to turn off an elevator or escalator during the day of rest.

Not only during Jesus's time was Sabbath strictly held, the Passover time was also solemn. The Jewish leaders were in the midst of one of the most important times of the year; thereby, heightening awareness for purity.[1] Women followers of Jesus were so conscious of the Sabbath that they did not finish preparing his body for burial (Luke 23:56), waiting till Sunday morning.[2] However, the religious leaders who had been threatened by

---

1. France, *Gospel of Matthew*, 1093, writes, "In this year, therefore, Friday was the day of preparation not only for the Sabbath but also for the chief day of the festival, so that the phrase 'the Preparation' does double duty."

2. These are the women in the Synoptic Gospels. John records Nicodemus and Joseph of Arimathea preparing the body with no indication that they did not finish. It is most likely they all were preparing the body together with the women leaving early for their own Sabbath preparations while Nicodemus and Joseph worked until closer to the

Jesus throughout his ministry could not let go and continued to be highly active despite the Sabbath and Passover.³ One issue that caused the leaders to want Jesus killed was his work on the Sabbath (Mark 3:1–6; Matt 12:1–14), but they themselves hypocritically ignored the strict regulations they imposed on others in order to assure their personal empires would be preserved (John 12:43).

Throughout the past nine days, one constant is the threatened religious leaders and the extremes they have gone to remove Jesus. Breaking commandments like thou shall not murder and bear false witnesses; now, they are desecrating the Sabbath. Blinded to their cold stubborn hearts, in their minds, they have changed the story in order to justify their actions. Rather than bowing down to the Messiah, they have produced in their minds that Jesus was a threat to the nation. One sign of cowardice is to construct a new narrative of what has happened instead of facing one's personal imperfections and repenting.

Going to Pilate

The chief priests and Pharisees approached Pilate again; highly concerned that Jesus's body might be removed. Their story: they were worried that the disciples would steal the corpse to perpetuate a myth, referring to him as the deceiver. In order to create this narrative of Jesus being a deceiver, they claimed his statements of rising on the third day were false (Matt 27:62–64). There is absolutely no hint in their tone that the idea of Jesus rising was an option. Their blindness to the truth continued as they worked on the Sabbath during the Passover. They needed close tabs on the body's whereabouts.

The Jews may have received information from Joseph of Arimathea that Jesus's body would be placed in Joseph's personal tomb, or Pilate may have told them the details after they approached him. Perhaps they wanted the body in a tomb so they could make sure that no one would steal it and asked Joseph to place Christ's body there, aware of the body's whereabouts. If wild animals ate the corpse, then his followers could say Jesus rose. After three days were concluded, they could leave Jesus's body in the wilderness

---

6:00 p.m. deadline of Sabbath activity.

3. Nolland, *Gospel of Matthew*, 1236, writes, "Is Matthew quietly saying that, unlike Joseph, the chief priests and the Pharisees here had failed to do the preparing they deemed necessary and are here found doing it on Sabbath, in violation of at least its spirit and probably, in their own best lights, also its letter?"

Breaking the Sabbath for Personal Security

for creatures to eat. Clearly the Jewish religious leaders were aware of the three-day resurrection claim and feared the dead Messiah would be taken.

Pilate was probably very tired of dealing with them and allowed the leaders to secure Jesus however they wanted (Matt 27:65).[4] Most likely temple guards were placed at Jesus's tomb, though a mixture of Roman soldiers is possible.[5] Jesus's tomb was sealed (Matt 27:66), most likely a "wax seal, to ensure that any attempt to open the tomb would be detectable."[6]

The fact that the leaders were so concerned about Jesus's body being stolen over honoring the Sabbath is another example of how they were more anxious about their personal empires than obeying the law. Sabbath regulations also mandated death if the rules were broken (Exod 31:14; 35:1–2; Num 15:32–36) but here, they totally disregarded whether or not they were honoring the Sabbath in order to safeguard their livelihood.

The Jewish religious leaders' vehemence to ensure Jesus's body was not stolen only adds to the grandeur that was about to come. No matter how hard humanity works to stop God's plan, nothing will prevent God from receiving glory. The religious leaders "held all the cards of earthly power, including access to the Roman governor, but despite all their efforts, they could not contain the Son of God."[7] Soon, Jesus would physically rise from the dead. The religious leaders' greatest fear became reality. Two thousand years later, people still follow him.

---

4. But some like Nolland, *Gospel of Matthew*, 1238–39, believe Pilate did dispatch Roman soldiers to guard Jesus's tomb. The Greek does not make it clear whether or not Pilate gave them a guard.

5. Based mainly on the fact that after the resurrection, the guards went straight to the priests and not Pilate, indicating these were temple guards and not Roman soldiers.

6. France, *Gospel of Matthew*, 1095n20.

7. Ibid., 1092.

Questions for Reflection and Group Discussion

Has there ever been a time where you were so blinded by fear, sin, pride, etc., that you did the wrong thing at the wrong time like the religious leaders?

1. What are consequences of doing the wrong thing at the wrong time?
2. Has there ever been a time in your life where you felt so threatened that it revealed deep insecurity?
3. How can security in God protect us from giving our heart away to our own personal fears and insecurity?
4. What are some areas in our life that could cause such blindness in our hearts? Is there a relationship you doubt? A job you are uncertain to take? A practice you are engaging in that may be unethical or ungodly?
5. What are areas in your life you think could become empires if not given to God?
6. How can meditating on the cross, resurrection, and second coming help us break down these empires?

22

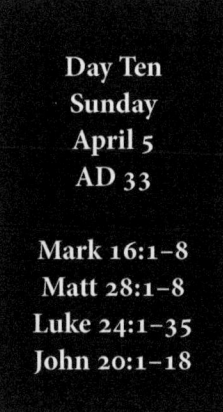

Day Ten
Sunday
April 5
AD 33

Mark 16:1–8
Matt 28:1–8
Luke 24:1–35
John 20:1–18

Easter Sunday, the Hope of the World

And if Christ has not been raised, then our preaching is in vain and your faith is in vain.

—1 CORINTHIANS 15:14

Easter was when Hope in person surprised the whole world by coming forward from the future into the present.

—N. T. WRIGHT

BILL HYBELS, FOUNDER AND senior pastor of Willow Creek Community Church in Barrington, Illinois, has stated: "The local church is the hope of the world," because God has entrusted to it the life-changing message of the gospel. If indeed the local church is the hope of the world then the hope of the church is its unyielding belief that Jesus rose from the dead. Indeed, the New Testament message of hope is based on Christ's resurrection.[1] On Easter Sunday Jesus rose from the dead and offered all of humanity the hope of the world, revitalizing with opportunity for a new life that was meant from the beginning.

We were designed to have hope as a pillar of emotional health. One of the most disparaging conditions is depression. Experts in the fields of psychology and psychiatry state that one of the main causes of depression is hopelessness.

Life is hard; Jesus's life was a perfect example. During these last ten days we have witnessed how cruel this world can be and how quickly things can turn. From being hailed as the Messianic King the previous Sunday to being crucified as a treasonous king just three days ago, Jesus's life depicts the great pain and hostility this world can manufacture. Without hope, it is very difficult to have a fulfilling life.

---

1. As well as his imminent return a second time.

An Empty Tomb

If there ever were a group who felt disheartened, it would be Jesus's followers, especially the remaining eleven. Peter was the most miserable; he had failed Jesus during his greatest time of need. Perhaps Peter was so beaten down that ending his life had crossed his mind. Tired, haggard, careworn, grieving, and sleep deprived while experiencing misery and emotional trauma, there was not a more despairing band of individuals in need of hope than Jesus's followers. It is not uncommon that we are at our lowest point before Christ raises us up.

After 6:00 p.m. Saturday evening, Mary Magdalene; Mary, the mother of James; Joanna; and Salome brought spices to finish preparing Jesus's body for burial (Mark 16:1; Luke 24:10).[2] It may have been too dark and late in the evening for all of them to trek over to Jesus's tomb, so, after buying the spices, they agreed to meet up very early Sunday morning (Mark 16:1).[3] Apparently, Mary Magdalene could not wait and went to Jesus's tomb first (John 20:1–2). She noticed that the tomb was empty and ran to tell John and Peter (John 20:2).[4] Upon hearing the news, both made a mad dash to the tomb, extremely late Saturday evening or even just past midnight

---

2. The discrepancies between the resurrection accounts have had much scholarly discussion. There is a special discrepancy between the Synoptics and John. There have been many avenues to reconcile the two, some state the gospel writers utilized different sources, see Keener, *Historical Jesus*, 330–32. Others state that John was writing the resurrection narrative from his own perspective and communicating his own theology. Dodd, *Fourth Gospel*, 444, writes, "I regard the Fourth Gospel as being in its essential character a theological work, rather than a history." Others believe John's history is superior to the Synoptics while others state that John's gospel is based on preaching; hence, the discrepancy while others believe John is supplementing the Synoptics. This section will be written from the perspective that John is supplementing the Synoptics. A good summary on the theories of John's resurrection narrative can be found in Brown, *Gospel according to John*, 996–1000.

3. In the remaining section, I am writing from the perspective that all the accounts are accurate, reconciling all four accounts into one. This presents significant challenges; many scholars hold to the gospel writers using different accounts of the resurrection to account for the discrepancies. Keener, *Historical Jesus*, 332, writes, "The various resurrection narratives in our Gospels vary considerably in length, focus, and detail. . . . It is hardly surprising that numerous accounts would exist and different Gospel writers would draw on different accounts."

4. Some reconcile the differences between the women and Mary Magdalene's visit based on Jesus's tomb having more than one chamber but two chambers. For the two chamber theory of Jesus's tomb, see Smith, *Tomb of Jesus*, 74–89.

Sunday.⁵ John arrived first (John 20:4). With the added responsibility of caring for Jesus's mother (John 19:26–27), he had to see if Mary's son's tomb was truly empty. Everything was happening fast. About thirty hours before, Jesus had been crucified and buried. The emotional grief and physical deprivation of the last few days had taken their toll on everyone, including John. He arrived at the tomb but did not go in. Peter was right behind him.

When Peter arrived, he immediately entered the tomb (John 20:6–7). Downtrodden over the events of Jesus's death, entering the tomb began to revive his soul. Both men are physically and emotionally exhausted. The last thirty some hours had brought on such great tiredness from sleep deprivation and such great emotional burden by the death of their friend and Lord, they are unable to wholly grasp what had happened (John 20:9). It was also dark, so they returned to the place where everyone was hiding. Most of the remaining eleven were either asleep or not willing to talk. Peter and John may also have gone to sleep; their visit may have given some hope and relief from stress to allow them to lie down, but they still did not fully grasp what was happening. Later, they would tell the disciples, but for now, events have overwhelmed them and they are processing these events while still in the midst of great emotional swings. It still did not make total sense (John 20:9), but soon would.

Mary Magdalene went back to the tomb after telling Peter and John (John 20:11), while the other women who bought spices were on their way (Luke 24:1).⁶ She is still weeping and grieving, too physically tired and emotionally drained to comprehend that Jesus indeed has risen. She was so shattered that not even the presence of angels, at first, frightens her, and interacts with them but is likely not even looking at their eyes, crying tears of grief over the loss of her master (John 20:12–13). Her tears will soon turn to joy. She is about to be reunited with her master.

---

5. Köstenberger and Taylor, *Final Days*, 182, state that John and Peter could have waited to rush to the tomb after the report of the women who talked with the angels in Luke 24:12. They argue that Mary Magdalene's report did not usher them to Jesus's tomb. This would make sense because the disciples' first reaction to the women's report was unbelief, which could have been Peter and John's first response. But the conjunction οὖν links John 20:3 with John 20:1–2 which would suggest that Mary's report was the impetus for their running. Also, John uses the same verb for "to run" (τρέχω) to describe Mary in 20:2 and in 20:4, Peter and John.

6. In John 20:2 Mary uses "we" which could be referring to the other women but the scene in John reads more like Mary was alone without them. Could this we be a reference to a gardener which she mentions in 20:15 (but in reality is the risen Christ)?

But she is now so distraught that when Jesus meets her at the tomb she does not recognize him, thinking he is a gardener (John 20:14–15). She still may have been weeping and not making eye contact, so emotionally drained that she could not recognize her master's voice. For some reason, she thinks his body has been taken and asks the supposed gardener if he had removed the body (John 20:14–15). She will soon find out he did not.

Infusion of Hope

After a brief interchange, Jesus told her it was he and Mary realizes it is indeed Jesus (John 20:16). Her deep sorry and physical tiredness began to vanish and her soul began to revive. All she felt now was joy as she saw her Lord risen; her first reaction was to embrace him tightly (John 20:17).[7] Jesus was also happy to see his dear follower renewed and tells her to share this good news amongst his disciples (John 20:17). Jesus knew his followers were dejected and had their interests and well-being as priorities.

While Mary was talking to Jesus, the other women continued on their way (Luke 24:1). As they were walking to the tomb, they expressed concerns about how the stone would be removed (Mark 16:3). The tomb would be sealed and difficult to budge. They assumed the stone would be too heavy for them, and there was no one to help them; perhaps the guards would refuse to open the tomb or even drive them away. They were unaware that the stone had already been removed and Jesus already appeared to Mary.

Upon arrival, the women were speechless when they saw the empty tomb. Mary was already there; unaware of where she was, overwhelmed by her interchange with Jesus. They all continued into the tomb with a joyfully pensive Mary to discover the two angels (Luke 24:4–6). Now Mary noticed the angels and was no longer dazed; the other women were alarmed when they saw the angels, but unlike the guards, they did not run. Jesus's words about his rising were going through their minds (Luke 24:7–8). Now their hopes were being realized.

One angel announced, "Jesus, who was crucified, has risen" and told the women to return and tell the disciples that the tomb was empty, especially Peter (Mark 16:6–7), who had not completely recovered from the

---

7. Some scholars hold to Jesus saying to Mary, "Do not hold onto me," as him preventing Mary from embracing him, but it is more likely that Mary is embracing, and Jesus, in a polite manner, is asking her to "let go."

shame of denying his Lord and experiencing Jesus's death. He had already seen the tomb, but it has still not sunk in that Jesus was alive (John 20:9).[8]

The angel said, "Why do you look for the living among the dead?" acknowledging Jesus was no longer in the tomb (Luke 24:5). The Savior was already on the move to Galilee and would later appear to his disciples. Afraid but hopeful, the women left the tomb and obeyed the angels' decree. By this time, Mary Magdalene tells the others she had already seen Jesus. Memories of his words filled all of their minds as they recalled him foretelling that he would rise from the dead (Luke 24:7).

But the other women, who did not talk to Jesus, were still overwhelmed and afraid; they needed encouragement (Mark 16:8). They would receive it when Jesus himself appeared to them. The trauma, stress, and sleep deprivation would now wane as the face of the risen Lord revived their spirits. Upon seeing his resurrected body, the women bowed down and worshipped (Matt 28:8–9). Their hearts were filled with overflowing. Three days earlier, on a Friday, they were overwhelmed with sorrow and anguish as they witnessed their innocent Lord brutally killed. They had given their entire lives to this man and now he was dead, but true to his word, Jesus was alive and revealed himself; he filled their hearts with hope and happiness. Emboldened by Jesus, they marched exuberantly to encourage his disciples.

Bribed Guards

Meanwhile, some of the guards ran to the city and told the chief priests what had happened (Matt 28:11–15). The guards, who were originally guarding Jesus's tomb, ran from fear. There would have been at least two, but most likely more. An earthquake, coupled with an angelic appearance, was more than enough to scatter them. They probably did not wait around to see Jesus walk out; terror would have gripped them so hard that their only reaction would be to run (Matt 28:4, 11). The guards' reaction was consistent in the Bible when humankind encounters the angelic; for example, after three weeks of praying, Daniel almost fell dead when confronted with an angelic figure (Dan 10:1—11:1). The guards are overcome with horror and ran for their lives.

---

8. Also, Mary's initial reaction when she discovered Jesus's body being removed maybe a clue to the readers that Peter also did not initially believe during the Johannine account of him and John visiting the tomb.

The protectors would have reported that an earthquake had occurred, and angels had arrived. This was the final opportunity for the Jewish leaders to bow down and worship Jesus as Messiah but instead of further investigation, blinded by their sin, they offered a large sum of money to the guards and filled them with a lie about Jesus's body being stolen. Assured of their safety, the guards were sent off (Matt 28:11–15).[9] Though they had witnessed the supernatural, the large sum of money poisoned their hearts; they forsook what they had seen to perpetuate the lie of Jesus's body being stolen. The Jewish leaders absolutely refused to acknowledge Jesus as Lord and this was their last chance. Some people love their personal empires so much that they would do anything to protect it.

All Eleven Hear

The women arrived to tell the Eleven that Jesus was no longer dead (Luke 24:9–12). His mother Mary was also likely among them. She is with John and the other disciples instead of the other women who went to her son's tomb. She may have been too distraught to even think about going; watching her child suffer had been too traumatic and she still needed time. Hope was about to fill her heart as the women arrived and proclaimed to the disciples that Jesus was alive. John may have already told Mary about her son's tomb being empty, but it was late when he returned, so she may have been sleeping or John may have been so sleep deprived and emotionally overloaded that he was processing and not ready to share what he had seen.

The disciples were still overcome by the pain of their master's death; the women's words initially sound like nonsense (Luke 24:11), except to Peter, who was already assimilating what he experienced. Maybe he felt the first time he went to the tomb was a dream; it would have been really late Saturday or past midnight on Sunday. He likely had not slept since the hours in Gethsemane, Thursday evening, when Jesus asked him to stay awake. He may have been in no good emotional and physical state to comprehend what he experienced. Perhaps he was able to get a little sleep and revive his body. His spirit would have received a jolt but just as with Mary Magdalene, the empty tomb might not have produced an initial response of belief. As soon as Peter heard the news from the women and especially Mary Magdalene, he ran to the tomb (Luke 24:12). After denying his Lord

---

9. The biblical account does not describe their final fate but it would not have been a surprise if they were later executed given the knowledge they possessed.

three times, Peter would run twice.[10] John had already gone and this news confirmed to him that what he saw was true (John 20:8); he would stay behind this time and explain to Mary what he had seen.

Upon arrival, Peter saw it was empty and went straight in (Luke 24:12). Visions of Jesus's face the night he denied him three times are piercing his heart but memories of Jesus stating he would rise from the dead were also in Peter's mind. Though he still was processing all that was happening (Luke 24:12), hope was being restored.

His initial experience at the tomb was probably similar to Mary's; he might not have thought Jesus had risen but this second visit proved to be one that restored his hope. His despair turned to joy. Somewhere during Peter's visit to the tomb or maybe on his way back, Jesus appeared to him (Luke 24:34; 1 Cor 15:5) and produced a joy that would fuel the rest of his life. Peter was clearly distraught and singled out by the Lord to be encouraged by the women (Mark 16:7) and now, the Lord himself has appeared to Simon Peter. This heart that was downtrodden and discouraged began to revive with great hope that would fuel his life for another thirty or more years of service and change the world. The searing event of Jesus rising from the dead and eventual restoration (John 21:15–23) would produce a faith so strong that when next confronted with death, Peter would not deny Jesus even once.

Emmaus Walk

Jesus did not appear only to the women and Peter; two others on their way to Emmaus, one named Cleopas, also experienced the risen Christ (Luke 24:13–35).[11] Jesus had just finished meeting with Mary Magdalene, the other women, and most likely Peter (Luke 24:33–34). Good Friday was still very fresh in everyone's minds. While talking, Jesus came up beside the two and asked them what they were discussing. It appears comedic. Cleopas could not believe this individual had no idea what had happened. All of Jerusalem—Jew and Gentile—were talking about Jesus. Cleopas referred to him as a prophet and not the Messiah. He had no idea he was sharing with the chosen one.

---

10. Peter running to Jesus's tomb twice would be a minority view. Some also believe Mary Magdalene visited Jesus's tomb three times.

11. The identity of the other individual is uncertain. Most think it was another man or his wife.

Jesus's death appeared to have dashed all hope for Cleopas that he was the Davidic king. It is clear that these two on their Emmaus walk were aware of the women's report of the risen Lord, but they did not believe. They even know of Peter and John's appearance at the tomb to confirm its emptiness, but still they do not believe and only viewed Jesus as a prophet (Luke 24:13–24). The Bible is clear that lack of faith is what upsets God and here were two who had the report of Jesus's return but did not have faith.

The Messiah's response was not meek; he said, "How foolish you are and how slow to believe all the prophets have spoken" (Luke 24:25). Despite his irritation, he knew that they were emotionally troubled over his death, and then patiently explained to them from the first five books of the Old Testament and the Prophets about himself (Luke 24:27). During this seven-mile journey from Jerusalem to Emmaus, their hearts were burning. They urged Jesus to stay. It was nearly evening and Jesus sat down to dine with them. As they broke the bread, their eyes were opened and they know it was the Lord himself.[12] Once Jesus knew they understood, he disappeared, knowing his purpose for spending so much time with them was accomplished (Luke 24:25–32). With hearts burning, they were eager to make the seven-mile journey back to Jerusalem to tell the disciples that it was true: Jesus was alive (Luke 24:32–35).

Soon, Jesus himself would appear to the disciples, but for now, their hearts were being prepared to accept this good news. The women had already told the disciples. Now, Cleopas and his companion appeared with hearts full of joy. Soon, the rest of the disciples who were downtrodden would be lifted up when Jesus himself appeared to them later that evening.[13]

The reports of Mary Magdalene; Mary the mother of James; Joanna; Salome; and Cleopas, and his companion would prepare this band of misfit disciples who did not fully comprehend him throughout his years of ministry. Their misunderstanding would turn to comprehension, and their despair would turn to joy; what once seemed hopeless now would produce a hope so great that almost all of them would die for their belief that Jesus was the risen Lord rather than recanting. Jesus's resurrection was a hope so strong that it fueled the remaining years of his followers' lives and should be a foundation of hope for our own.

---

12. On the issue the meal as a scene of restored fellowship between Jesus and his followers, see Garland, *Luke*, 956 and nn23–25.

13. All except Thomas, who is not present on Easter with the disciples but in a week, will experience the risen Lord for himself.

Easter Sunday, the Hope of the World

Questions for Personal Reflection or Group Discussion

What are some things you have hoped for?

1. What are some things you wished for that ended up dashing your hope?
2. Has there been a time when you wanted to give up but something kept you going?
3. How is Jesus's resurrection a pillar of our hope?
4. How can we think more of the resurrected Christ?
5. For Paul, if Jesus did not rise again, Christianity is worthless (1 Cor 15). How can the resurrection help us when we doubt? Struggle?

23

Easter Evening Commission

If you take missions out of the Bible, you won't have anything left but the covers.

—NINA GUNTER

Therefore go and make disciples of all nations.

—MATTHEW 28:19

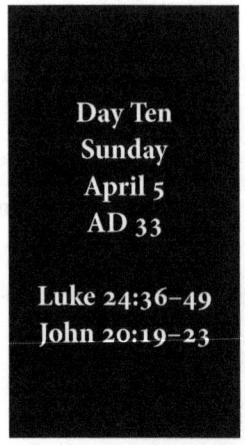

Day Ten
Sunday
April 5
AD 33

Luke 24:36–49
John 20:19–23

WHEN PEOPLE THINK OF Easter, their first thoughts are of Jesus rising early in the morning. Rightly so! Without Christ rising, the Apostle Paul in 1 Corinthians 15 says the Christian faith is worthless. To commemorate this early morning event, churches have sunrise services that end with a breakfast. Then, people often go out to Sunday Easter brunch. The holiday is often synonymous with morning celebration. What is often neglected as we think of Easter Sunday is a significant event that very night: an Easter evening commission.[1]

Jesus Appears to the Disciples

The door was locked for fear of the Jewish leaders who killed Jesus.[2] Their Master died on a Friday and three days later, the threat was still very forceful. The Sanhedrin was gloating because the schemers thought their plan had succeeded, but they are still wary that Jesus's disciples could cause trouble; hence, the locked door. Mary Magdalene and company had already told them Jesus was no longer dead and Cleopas had the news confirmed

---

1. Most commonly referred to as "the great commission," most associate this term with Matt 28:19–20. All four gospels contain a commission, but Mark 16:15 reads: "And he said to them, 'Go into all the world and proclaim the gospel to the whole creation.'" But many scholars do not consider the longer ending of Mark (16:9–20) as part of the original gospel.

2. Morris, *Luke*, 359, states that the scenes in Luke and John are the same event.

Easter Evening Commission

(Luke 24:9–11, 33–35); despite their testimony the disciples were not able to comprehend what was happening (Luke 24:11). But that would change soon and they would know the full truth.

Despite the locked door, Jesus was able to walk right through it and materialize before his followers (Luke 24:36). In a resurrected and glorified body, Jesus is no longer the Suffering Servant; he had accomplished that task on the cross. He was now fully the Davidic King and appeared to the disciples much as he had to Peter, James, and John during the transfiguration (Mark 9:2–13; Matt 17:1–9; Luke 9:28–36). John 20:19–23: Jesus came and stood in their midst saying,

> "Peace be with you." And when He had said this, He showed them both His hands and His side. The disciples then rejoiced when they saw the Lord. So Jesus said to them again, "Peace be with you; as the Father has sent Me, I also send you." And when He had said this, He breathed on them and said to them, "Receive the Holy Spirit. If you forgive the sins of any, their sins have been forgiven them; if you retain the sins of any, they have been retained."

The disciples were startled at first, thinking they saw a ghost and asking: "Who is this man in our midst?"[3] But they were reassured after they had seen Jesus's hands (likely wrists),[4] his side (Luke 24:39–40), and heard his request for food; they no longer feared him being a ghost (Luke 24:41).[5] The disciples were still struggling to believe because they were overwhelmed with joy (Luke 24:41). Their souls had been restored and they had moved from despair to jubilation.

On Friday they had watched their Master die and were unable to care for his body. A band of women along with two Jewish religious leaders did. On Saturday, they were in hiding because of their association with Jesus, fearful that the Jewish leaders would try to kill them along with their teacher. Sunday evening, the disciples were revived, their hope returned as they saw their Master risen and glorified.

Then Jesus uttered an Easter evening commission in John 20:21: the sent one (Jesus) now sends his disciples to tell the world about him. Both

---

3. Some argue that those present like Cleopas, who had already experienced the risen Lord should not have been startled but a sudden appearance through locked doors would startle anyone. Some believe Peter was among the disciples to whom Jesus appeared but we know Thomas was not, so the reference to the Eleven would not mean all were present.

4. See Carson, *Gospel according to John*, 656.

5. See also Morris, *Luke*, 360.

Matt 28:18–20[6] and John 20:21 make references to the triune godhead. Matthew's Trinitarian reference emphasizes evangelism when the call is to baptize in the name of the Father, Son, and Holy Spirit, and then discipleship: "teaching them to obey my commandments." In John 20, the Father is the one who sent Jesus; therefore, he is now sending his disciples and gives them the Holy Spirit[7] to help them in their "sending" that he so eloquently expounded in John 14–17.[8] Luke has his version of the "Easter Evening Commission," stating:[9] "This is what is written: The Messiah will suffer and rise from the dead on the third day, and repentance for the forgiveness of sins will be preached in his name to all nations, beginning at Jerusalem" (Luke 24:46–47). Jesus did not encourage his followers to continue hiding out for safety but to be prepared to proclaim his death, resurrection, and repentance for forgiveness of sins to all nations beginning in Jerusalem. Jesus's early morning resurrection led to a late evening commission: tell the world that Jesus has conquered sin and death, and through belief in the Savior, there is life eternal.[10]

They could not fulfill this commission with their own power; they needed power from on high: "And behold, I am sending the promise of my Father upon you. But stay in the city until you are clothed with power from on high" (Luke 24:49). It was the Holy Spirit who would empower them to fulfill this commission.[11]

The disciples' despair turned into hope and joy as they witnessed the risen Lord. This hope and joy would lead most of them to die martyrs' deaths in foreign lands, taking the good news that Jesus had died for our sins and risen from the dead. This is the message those who follow him today must proclaim.[12]

---

6. Most hold that this version of the great commission was given later than Easter evening.

7. See Whitacre, *John*, 480–82, on the Holy Spirit and his function in the community of believers.

8. Whitacre writes, "Over forty times throughout the Gospel, Jesus is said to have been sent by God, and now that will become characteristic of his disciples also" (ibid., 479).

9. Some hold to these words being spoken near the end of Jesus's forty days after the resurrection. See Köstenberger and Taylor, *Final Days*, 192–93.

10. Whitacre, *John*, 479, writes, "Mission is at the heart of discipleship."

11. See Morris, *Luke*, 362, and Carson, *Gospel according to John*, 649–55.

12. See also Whitacre, *John*, 479–81, on how John 20:19–23 impacts the nature and mission of the church.

Easter Evening Commission

In the last event of Jesus's ten days, we see the king authorizing his disciples to tell the world about himself. Ten days ago, Jesus traveled from Ephraim to Bethany, then walked from Bethany to Jerusalem on Sunday through Thursday, from Jerusalem to Gethsemane four days ago, from Gethsemane to Golgotha then to heaven three days ago, and returned to Jerusalem in a resurrected body today. He walked the earth another forty days where he subdued the doubt of Thomas, caught 153 fish for Peter, and would have breakfast with his followers on the beach, before saying goodbye on a mountain in Bethany and returning to heaven. But someday, he will return (Acts 1:11).

The hope of the resurrected Christ coupled with the Easter evening commission drove his followers for the next generation where almost all of them would die violently in a foreign land, proclaiming his death, resurrection, repentance, and belief; choosing to lose their lives for the message of Jesus. They had tasted the goodness of the Lord and given up all for his glory. They believed they would see Jesus again in their lifetime; that belief gave force to their proclamation of the Easter message to the whole world. All died without seeing his second coming, but they were greeted by him in paradise. The church is still in this waiting pattern where Christ's return is imminent and close. No one except the Father knows when that time will arrive (Mark 13:32; Matt 24:36), but it will come and we, his current followers must be ready. In the meantime, the message of the gospel must be proclaimed to everyone in the entire world so they can have a chance to meet the risen Lord and experience for themselves the life of Christ.

Through his final ten days, we have seen that Jesus experienced so much because of his great love (1 John 4:19; John 3:16; John 15:9), and gave us many lessons to live by. May these lessons fuel a spirit of service, devotion, study, and worship for the rest of our days before we meet him in heaven.

Questions for Reflection and Group Discussion

How often do you think of Easter and the hope of the resurrection?

1. How could daily and consistently thinking of the resurrection and second coming of the Lord change our lives and outlook?
2. The fact that most of the disciples died in a foreign land because of the message of Easter should tell us what about the gospel?
3. How important is evangelism and missions in your life currently? How does Jesus's Easter evening commission affect you and your church?
4. What stood out to you when you read Jesus's Easter evening commission?
5. How will you apply Jesus's Easter evening commission to your life?
6. How can Jesus's Easter evening commission change our lives right now?

Appendix 1

A Bracketed Bethany Anointing

MICHAEL CHUNG

> *All four Gospels contain an anointing scene of Jesus. Most acknowledge Luke's anointing scene as separate from Matthew, Mark, and John's, the later three recording the same event. Matthew's anointing scene appears to be an abridgment of Mark's. When comparing Mark's version against John's, challenges arise. In this article, I will argue that John is influenced by the Markan account's use of the literary device intercalation. When this is applied to John's anointing pericope, non-corresponding details are more coherent.*
>
> *Key Words: Intercalation; Anointing; John 12:1-11; Mark 14:1-11; Mark's influence on John*

THERE ARE NOT TOO many scenes of Jesus's life outside of Passion Week that are chronicled by all four gospel writers; one is his anointing (Mark 14:3–9; Matt 26:6–13; Luke 7:36–50; John 12:1–11). J. K. Elliott states that all four evangelists recording the anointing makes it "on the same level as the miraculous feedings or the crucifixion."[1] The similarities, differences, and nature between the accounts of Jesus's anointing have been the subject of scholarly dialogue.[2] The range is wide and the following list is not exhaustive, but most will agree that the anointing accounts are on a continuum or a derivative of: (1) The writers' use of the oral and/or written tradition(s)

---

1. Elliott, *Anointing*, 105.

2. There are many who have done comparative studies between the four anointing scenes, some noteworthy are: Sabbe, *Anointing of Jesus*, 2051–82; Collins and Attridge, *Mark*, 622–25; Moule, *Gospel according to Mark*, 112; Brown, *Gospel according to John*, 449–52; Culpepper, *Gospel and Letters of John*, 190–93; Kurek-Chomycz, *Fragrance*, 344–51.

Appendix 1

where the gospel writers may have used different components of the traditions[3] (2) Because of the traditions, one occurrence of Jesus being anointed actually occurred and the gospel writers are reflecting the same event.[4] (3) There are two distinct anointing stories.[5]

In comparing anointing accounts, Raymond Brown and others do not think it is necessary to hold Matthew's account separate,[6] arguing that Matthew's anointing version is an abridgement of Mark's.[7] For the purposes

---

3. Dodd, *Historical Tradition*, 162–73, writes, "Variations arose in the course of oral transmission" (quote at 172). Gardner-Smith, *Synoptic Gospels*; Sanders, *Historical Jesus*, 127. On the issue of John using alternative sources, Kurek-Choycz, *Fragrance*, 348, writes,
> The proposals of those who put forward alternative sources of John's account, at least with respect to John 12:1–8, are not particularly compelling. Curiously, even though everyone agrees that the anointing accounts are of extreme importance for determining the relationship between John and the Synoptics, the discussion in some of the contributions aimed at demonstrating John's independence of the other Gospels gives the impression that the preconceived result guides them more than common sense. While they play down obvious similarities, they tend to exaggerate even minor differences.

See also Reinbold, *Der älteste Bericht über den Tod Jesu*, 73–78, 92–215, for discussion of John and Mark using different revisions of the same written tradition.

4. See Sabbe, *Anointing*, 2051–82, who suggests that John could be a redaction of the two Synoptic accounts; Elliott, *Anointing of Jesus*, 105–7; Van Til, *Three Anointings*, 73–82; Holst, "One Anointing of Jesus," 435–46, 436, 446, writes, "Careful and consistent application of the form-critical method leads me to conclude that C. H. Dodd and others are correct when they maintain that the four accounts deal with only one incident. . . . The application of form-critical methods shows that it is tenable to maintain that one story or incident lies behind the anointing stories in the four Gospels." Dodd, *Historical Tradition*, 162–73. Kurek-Choycz, *Fragrance*, 346, notes the discussion of Luke 7:36–50 in Delobel, *L'onction par la pécheresse*, 415–75, as citing one source for the anointing accounts.

5. Keener, *Gospel of John*, 2:860; Legault, *Form-Critical Method*, 131–41; Bock, *Luke*, 690; France, *Gospel of Matthew*, 973; Nolland, *Commentary on the Gospel of Luke*, 352; Evans, *Mark 8:27—16:20*, 359; Witherington, *John's Wisdom*, 207; Green and Hearon, *Anointing*, 13, in which they state that Mark and Matthew are one account, Luke is a separate one, and John is a "conflation of the two." Many consider Mark 14:3–9, Matt 26:1–16, and John 12:3–8 being the same story and Luke 7:36–50 being a separate account, cf. Coakley, *Anointing*, 241–56.

6. Claim of authorship is not being made when using proper names like Matthew, Mark, and John.

7. Brown, *Gospel according to John*, 449; see also Davies and Allison, *Critical and Exegetical Commentary*, 441; Hendrickson, *Exposition of the Gospel of Mark*, 557, writes, "John (12:1–8) is by far the most detailed, with 142 words in the original. Mark (14:3–9) comes next, with 124 words. The shortest is Matthew (26:6–13) with only 109. The difference consists to a large extent in the material which Mark and/or John add(s) to Matthew's summary."

of this article, the dominant focus will be on the pericope of John 12:1–11 with Mark 14:1–11 as its primary counterpart.

One issue is: "Where does the anointing pericope in John begin and end?" Scholars are not unified. Some think the pericope encompasses John 12:1–8,[8] while others will lengthen to 11:55—12:8,[9] or 11:55—12:11,[10] and even as lengthy as 11:55—12:19.[11] There are others holding to this article's pericope of John 12:1–11.[12]

Another issue arises: chronology. The Markan account differs from the one in John's Gospel. Mark 14:1 indicates the anointing happened two days before the Passover while scholars link John 12:3–8 to John 12:1 indicating six days.[13] Mark has placed his account after the triumphal entry of Jesus into Jerusalem while it *appears* John records his account before Jesus's Jerusalem entry. Ben Witherington writes, "In terms of historical probabilities, it seems more likely that the Bethany episode preceded the triumphal entry as the Johannine account has it, rather than the order we find in Mark."[14] On this issue, there are those who take a position advocating that John is the one historically correct, being more reliable than Mark (or other Synoptics), as

---

8. Esler and Piper, *Lazarus, Mary, and Martha*, 52; Keener, *Gospel of John*, 859; Beasley-Murray, *John*, 208; Morris, *Gospel according to John*, 571; Lindars, *Gospel of John*, 412; Culpepper, *Gospel and Letters of John*, 191; Brown, *Gospel according to John*, 447.

9. Ridderbos, *Gospel according to John*, 411.

10. Malina and Rohrbaugh, *John*, 204; Barrett, *Gospel according to St. John*, 408; Whitacre, *John*, 299.

11. Michaels, *Gospel of John*, 659.

12. Witherington, *John's Wisdom*, 206. See also Carson, *Gospel according to John*, 425.

13. Brown, *Gospel according to John*, 452, writes, "Mark's account of the Bethany scene seems to be dated two days before Passover. We say 'seems' because no date appears in the actual Marcan account of the anointing (xiv 3–9) but only in the context (xiv 1). . . . Mark and Matthew place the scene considerably after Jesus's entrance into Jerusalem (Mark xi 1–10)." Moloney, *Gospel of Mark*, 279, writes, "Even within the Markan account, the chronology can be difficult to follow. Most likely the 'two days' mentioned here would mean twenty-four hours, as a day was counted on each appearance of daylight. The evening of one day and the morning of the next would be 'two days' . . . anointing (Wednesday)." But Moloney's chronology may have some challenges; it does not take into account that there likely is a Sabbath on Wednesday before Passover begins. There are special Sabbaths during the Jewish lunar calendar year and the one observed on Wednesday before Passover is likely *Shabbat HaGadol*, also known as the Great Sabbath.

14. Witherington, *John's Wisdom*, 207.

demonstrated by Witherington's above statement.[15] Others advocate John's dependence on the Synoptics (with some focusing on Mark).[16]

In this article, I will argue the writer of John's Gospel is using a literary device known as intercalation[17]—where one pericope is sandwiched in between another—to add emphasis to the overall message of the Jewish leaders' desire to kill Lazarus. I will also argue that the writer of John's use of intercalation is influenced by the writer of Mark's application of it in Mark 14:1–11. If John 12:1–11 is indeed an intercalation, then discussion areas like chronology, pericope parameters, etc., can be abetted.

Since there is no record of Lazarus's name after John 12:17 and the majority of his New Testament references are in conjunction with Jesus raising him from the dead,[18] there is no biblical account of his second death. John, likely writing after Lazarus has died, could be communicating to the reader the type of death Lazarus would have experienced similar to that of Jesus: precipitated by the Jewish religious leaders. We will first look at the "Lazarus Sections" of John 12:1–2 and 12:9–11.

---

15. See Robinson, *John*; see also Coakley, *Anointing*, 241–56; Coakley writes, "In short, John's setting is preferable to Mark's" (243). Taylor, *Gospel according to Mark*, 53; Witherington, *John's Wisdom*, 207; Fortna, *Gospel of Signs*, 152; Howard, *Fourth Gospel*, 151.

16. Van Belle, *What We Have Heard*, 325–37, espousing the Leuven Hypothesis: the Gospel of John is dependent on the Synoptics. For the relationship between John and Mark, see Smith, *John among the Gospels*, and Bauckham, *John for Mark*, 147–72.

17. Shepherd, *Markan*, 4, states that intercalation can also be known as interpolation, framing, bracketing, and sandwiching. See also von Dobschütz, *Zur Erzählerkunst des Markus*, 193–98; Malick, "Examination of Jesus's View of Women," 4–15. For a good summary of the literature review of intercalation and discussion of its nature as a whole, see Shepherd, *Markan*, 4–18, 27–31. In addition to literature, the term *intercalation* is also used in other fields like chemistry, university administration, biochemistry, timekeeping in regards to calendars, and medicine, to name a few. All use the term in relation to "insertions" of various forms.

18. It is highly unlikely that the Lazarus mentioned in Luke 16:19–31 is the same Lazarus of John 11 and 12. Esler and Piper, *Lazarus, Mary, and Martha*, 50–52, draw some interesting conclusions comparing the Lazarus of Luke with the Johannine Lazarus coming to a similar conclusion as Coakley, *Anointing*, 255, who writes, "The parable of the rich man and Lazarus (16:19–31), whether authentic or not, seems to depend on the story of Lazarus's resurrection and not vice versa."

A Bracketed Bethany Anointing

WAS IT NECESSARY TO SEPARATE THE "LAZARUS SECTIONS" INTO 12:1–2 AND 12:9–11?

John 12:1–11 has an unusual turn and return. In this section, Lazarus is clearly the focal point of 12:1–2 and returns in 12:9–11 while totally removed from 12:3–8. Raymond Brown already suspects the pericope possesses something unusual:

> The Lazarus story was brought into its present chronological sequence rather late . . . we regard the present localization of the Lazarus story as secondary, . . . an editorial attempt to tie chs. xi and xii together. It is obvious that they (Lazarus and Martha) have no important role in the scene of the anointing.[19]

Raymond Brown also states the mentioning of Lazarus in the John 12 pericope as "awkward."[20] Could intercalation show Lazarus's importance, mitigating the awkwardness?

Scott Brown writes, "Intercalation is a means of conspicuously juxtaposing two episodes or pericopae. This close structural relationship calls attention to any overt similarities, contrasts, or formal parallels that these episodes share."[21] This literary device is best thought of in terms of a sandwich, where one section is thrust right in the middle of another.[22] One characteristic of the literary device of intercalation is that when the middle (inner) story is removed and the outer story is connected to the previous outer pericope, it reads as one flowing unit. This is one of the eight

---

19. Brown, *Gospel according to John*, 447n1, 452–53, brackets mine. Though Martha's role in the scene is not as significant as Mary's, we will see below that her actions do contrast with Mary's (as they have in Luke 10:38–42 and John 11:20–33) to assist the pericope's use of intercalation.

20. Brown, *Gospel according to John*, 453.

21. Brown, *Mark 11:1—12:12*, 78.

22. Edwards, "Markan Sandwiches," 197, writes (Edwards uses interpolation instead of intercalation but has the same meaning):
> Interpolation concerns a larger (usually narrative) unit of material consisting of two episodes or stories which are narrated in three paragraphs or pericopes. The whole follows an A1–B–A2 schema, in which the B-episode forms an independent unit of material, whereas the flanking A-episodes require one another to complete their narrative. The B-episode consists of only one story; it is not a series of stories, nor itself so long that the reader fails to link A2 with A1. Finally, A2 normally contains an allusion at its beginning, which refers back to A1, e.g., repetition of a theme, proper nouns, etc.

Appendix 1

characteristics of intercalation espoused by Tom Shepherd: "An ellipsis of the outer story occurs across the inner story."[23]

One of the most common examples of intercalation found in the New Testament is the passage from Mark 11:12–23 where Jesus curses the fig tree and in between—Mark 11:15–19—cleanses the temple. If one removed Mark 11:15–19, and linked Mark 11:12–14 with Mark 11:20–23, it would form a logically flowing account:

Mark 11:12–14, 20–23: "On the following day, when they came from Bethany, he was hungry. And seeing in the distance a fig tree in leaf, he went to see if he could find anything on it. When he came to it, he found nothing but leaves, for it was not the season for figs. And he said to it, 'May no one ever eat fruit from you again.' And his disciples heard it. . . . As they passed by in the morning, they saw the fig tree withered away to its roots. And Peter remembered and said to him, 'Rabbi, look! The fig tree that you cursed has withered.' And Jesus answered them, 'Have faith in God. Truly, I say to you, whoever says to this mountain, "Be taken up and thrown into the sea," and does not doubt in his heart, but believes that what he says will come to pass, it will be done for him.'"

As one reads the story of the withered/cursed fig tree, it reads as if there is not another section in between Mark 11:14 to 11:20, a "flow" marks the two back-to-back fragments as one portion. Applying this same technique to the pericope of John 12:1–11 and removing the section where Mary of Bethany anoints Jesus feet would produce a similar flowing narrative:

John 12:1–2, 9–11: Six days before the Passover, Jesus therefore came to Bethany, where Lazarus was, whom Jesus had raised from the dead. So they gave a dinner for him there. Martha served, and Lazarus was one of those reclining with him at the table. When the large crowd of the Jews learned that Jesus was there, they came, not only on account of him but also to see Lazarus, whom he had raised from the dead. So the chief priests made plans to put Lazarus to death as well, because on account of him many of the Jews were going away and believing in Jesus.

Putting the two "Lazarus sections" together would produce a movement that would not need 12:3–8, fulfilling the ellipsis of the outer story through the inner story.[24] We can already see evidence of intercalation from the above discussion of Shepherd's eighth characteristic applied to John

---

23. Shepherd, *Markan Sandwich*, 327. See also Malick, "Examination of Jesus's View of Women," 9n2.

24. Shepherd, *Markan Sandwich*, 327.

12:1–11.²⁵ Shepherd offers seven more features of intercalation which will be applied to John 12:1–11.²⁶

*Characteristic 1: Apart from initial focalization, the outer story is the temporal border of the inner story.*²⁷

There is a clear temporal border of the outer story of Lazarus with the inner story of Mary anointing Jesus. John 12:1–2, 9–11 unequivocally focuses on Lazarus while his name is not even mentioned in the inner story of Jesus being anointed by Mary (and Judas's disapproval of the anointing). Lazarus is mentioned twice in 12:1–2: Ὁ οὖν Ἰησοῦς πρὸ ἓξ ἡμερῶν τοῦ πάσχα ἦλθεν εἰς Βηθανίαν, ὅπου ἦν Λάζαρος, ὃν ἤγειρεν ἐκ νεκρῶν Ἰησοῦς ἐποίησαν οὖν αὐτῷ δεῖπνον ἐκεῖ, καὶ ἡ Μάρθα διηκόνει, ὁ δὲ Λάζαρος εἷς ἦν ἐκ τῶν ἀνακειμένων σὺν αὐτῷ. There is no mention of Lazarus's name in 12:3–8 but in 12:9–10 (11), Lazarus again appears two times: Ἔγνω οὖν [ὁ] ὄχλος πολὺς ἐκ τῶν Ἰουδαίων ὅτι ἐκεῖ ἐστιν καὶ ἦλθον οὐ διὰ τὸν Ἰησοῦν μόνον, ἀλλ' ἵνα καὶ τὸν Λάζαρον ἴδωσιν ὃν ἤγειρεν ἐκ νεκρῶν ἐβουλεύσαντο δὲ οἱ ἀρχιερεῖς ἵνα καὶ τὸν Λάζαρον ἀποκτείνωσιν(providing a clear temporal border to the inner story. Mary's name is not mentioned in the outer story.

Raymond Brown found the reference to Lazarus in John 12 "awkward,"²⁸ but once intercalation is applied, Brown's issue should be ameliorated.

---

25. Edwards, "Markan Sandwiches," 196, writes that intercalation (again, he uses interpolation)
> is, to be sure, a literary technique, but its purpose is theological; that is, the sandwiches emphasize the major motifs of the Gospel, especially the meaning of faith, discipleship, bearing witness, and the dangers of apostasy. Moreover, I shall endeavor to show that the middle story nearly always provides the key to the theological purpose of the sandwich. The insertion interprets the flanking halves. To use the language of medicine, the transplanted organ enlivens the host material.

26. Shepherd, *Markan Sandwich*, 327.

27. Ibid., 327. On the issue of intercalation and ancient literature outside the New Testament, see Edwards, "Markan Sandwiches," 200–203, where he writes, "There are many examples in ancient literature where an author interrupts one story with another in order to achieve a desired effect" (200). Edwards discusses intercalation in places *The Odyssey*, *Iliad*, 2, Macc, Hos 1–3, and 2 Sam 11:1—12:25. See also Malick, "Examination of Jesus's View of Women," 9n4; Downing, *Nativity*, 105–17, where he has discussed parallels with Hellenistic and Roman histories, lives, comedies in the theater, and romances; Magnes, *Sense and Absence*, 1986, compares Mark with Homer, Vergil, Philostratus, and Xenophon; Robbins, *Summons and Outline in Mark*, 97–114, the Gospel of Mark with Greco-Roman literature.

28. Brown, *Gospel according to John*, 453.

Appendix 1

Characteristic 2: There is a unique pattern of focalization and defocalization of the two stories, which includes incomplete defocalization of the outer story at the point where breakaway occurs to the inner story. This creates a "gap" for the outer story across the inner story.[29]

As has been demonstrated above, there does exist an incomplete defocalization of the outer story at the point where Mary enters in 12:3. The scene shifts rapidly from (ὁ δὲ Λάζαρος εἷς ἦν ἐκ τῶν ἀνακειμένων) Lazarus reclining at the table, (12:2) to ('Η οὖν Μαριὰμ λαβοῦσα λίτραν μύρου νάρδου πιστικῆς πολυτίμου) Mary taking a pint of pure nard (12:3).

The string of ἡ οὖν in 12:3 is unique to John—also present in John 11:20, 32; 18:12—with no other appearances in the New Testament. Each time the string appears there is a transition from one character to another, which would aid the focalization and defocalization of the two stories.

When the story picks up in 12:9, Lazarus is now the focal point of attention again as the object of the crowd's curiosity and the object of the Jewish religious leaders' angst.

Characteristic 3: A new character or newly named character is noted at the reentry into the outer story.[30]

12:1-2 has Jesus and Lazarus as the focal point characters while Jesus and Mary (and Judas) are the primary actors in 12:3-8. Upon reentry at 12:9, the new character of "the great crowd of Jews" (Ἰο`Ð o;cloj polu.j evk tw/n VIoudai,wn) appears that was not present in 12:1-2, or 12:3-8. The chief priests (oi` avrcierei/j) are also introduced as those who are plotting to kill like they are in the Synoptics, but in this case, Lazarus is added to their murderous desires.

Characteristic 4: Active character crossover does not occur between the two stories, except for Jesus.[31]

Except for Jesus, Mary is not mentioned in 12:1-2 or 12:9-11 while Lazarus is not present during Mary's anointing of Jesus's feet in 12:3-8. Hence, Raymond Brown's struggle as to why the writer of John included Lazarus in the first place.[32] With the characters not crossing over as characteristic of intercalation, this can help answer Brown's question as to the priority of Lazarus associated with the anointing scene.

---

29. Shepherd, *Markan Sandwich*, 327.
30. Ibid.
31. Ibid.
32. Brown, *Gospel according to John*, 447, 452–53

A Bracketed Bethany Anointing

Characteristic 5: Parallel actions are done by contrasting groups or contrasting actions are done by parallel groups in the two stories.[33]

Contrasting action occurs, while Lazarus is at the table with Jesus and likely reclining in a relaxed position, Mary is wiping Jesus's feet with her hair in a prostrate position of worship and service. Lazarus is the object of the Jewish leaders plot for death due to his miracle story of resurrection while Mary is preparing Jesus for death (and in some ways, Lazarus too) with her anointing Jesus with perfume.

Also, Martha serves the meal while Mary and wipes Jesus's feet. Both are actions but Martha is practicing hospitality while Mary is practicing worship.

Characteristic 6: The outer story has an elliptical action which crosses the inner story and contrasts with the actions of the inner story.[34]

Similar to the previous characteristic, Jesus is with Lazarus at the table, experiencing a dinner in his honor in 12:1–2, and is still. Lazarus is mentioned twice as being raised from the dead (12:1, 9) and is the object of the Jewish leaders plot to have Lazarus killed due to many people following Jesus on account of the miracle. By contrast, Mary will anoint Jesus, also influenced by the miracle of her brother's resurrection but instead of plotting to kill Jesus, she worships him. Mary is also actively wiping Jesus's feet while Lazarus is reclining.

Characteristic 7: The plots of the two stories interlink following a turn-return pattern.[35]

Certainly the two stories interlink as the turn goes from Lazarus and Jesus to Mary and Jesus then back to Lazarus and Jesus. The plot of Lazarus being raised from the dead as the impetus for him being the target of murder by the Jewish religious leaders (12:1, 10–11) interlinks with Mary's anointing story of preparing Jesus for burial (12:3, 7–8). Lazarus is also the targeted for death by the Jewish religious leaders due to his miraculous resurrection. Jesus, in the inner story, is also being prepared to die at the hands of the Jewish leaders because he has been doing signs that make the religious leaders' followers depart their allegiance which is pledged to Jesus.

As we have compared the pericope of John 12:1–11 with Shepherd's eight characteristics of intercalation in narrative function, there is a pattern

---

33. Shepherd, *Markan Sandwich*, 327.
34. Ibid.
35. Ibid.

APPENDIX 1

that John's anointing scene in 12:1–11 matches Shepherd's Markan intercalation findings, pointing to John also using the literary device in his pericope.

JOHN'S FAMILIARITY WITH MARK

The issue of John's dependence and/or independence on Mark and the Synoptic Gospels has been in much deliberation.[36] Though many agree that John used Mark[37] there exists a spectrum, as touched on earlier, ranging from John being independent of Mark;[38] to the writer of John expecting most of his readers to know Mark;[39] to the writer of John being totally dependent on the Gospel of Mark.[40] At the very least, as Carson suggests, "John had read Mark."[41] However, as Esler and Piper pronounce, the question on John's dependence and independence on Mark (or Synoptics in general) is "not proven."[42] Most scholars will acknowledge that John was written later[43] so John's readers could have been familiar with Mark since

---

36. One of the many good discussions can be found in Carson, *Gospel according to John*, 49–58. See also Collins and Attridge, *Mark*, 622–25; Blomberg, *Historical Reliability of the Gospels*, 196–204, and his work, *Historical Reliability of John's Gospel*, 44–54.

37. E.g., Sabbe, *Anointing*, 2053. Sabbe uses both Matthew and Mark in comparison with John but emphasizes Mark.

38. E.g., Barnett, *Logic of History*, 104–5, writes, "Careful comparison of the texts of Mark and John indicate that neither of these Gospels is dependent on the other. Yet they have a number of incidents in common: For example, . . . the burial of Jesus in the tomb of Joseph of Arimathea." Keener, *Gospel of John*, 861, believes John uses an independent tradition and does not rely on the Synoptics but acknowledges that John's audience "already knows a form of the tradition in which the person who anointed Jesus was Mary." See also Sanders, *Those Whom Jesus Loved*, 29–41; Goodenough, *Primitive Gospel*, 152–55; Holst, "One Anointing of Jesus," 435–46, 443, believes Luke is the most primitive anointing account; März, *Zur Traditionsgeschichte von Mk 14*, 106–11; Legault, *Form-Critique Method*, 131–45; Coakley, *Anointing*.

39. See Carson, *Gospel according to John*, 51; Bauckham, *John for Mark*, 148; Barrett, *Gospel according to St. John*, 390, believes John "is able to presuppose that his readers were already familiar with it (anointing story); this implies that they were Christians and knew the Synoptic tradition."

40. One can also add the Synoptics in general to this continuum. There is also discussion that the evangelists are dependent on each other, see Kurek-Choycz, *Fragrance*, 348; Schweizer, *Good News*, 288; Schnackenburg, *Bethanien*, 49.

41. Carson, *Gospel according to John*, 51.

42. Esler and Piper, *Lazarus, Mary and Martha*, 55; they also discuss other Synoptics like Luke. For discussion of John's dependence on Luke, see Coakley, *Anointing*, 250–52; Coakley advocates Johannine priority.

43. Bauckham, *Jesus and the Eyewitnesses*, 243, believes that Mark's Passion account is

A Bracketed Bethany Anointing

Jesus's anointing is present in all three Synoptic Gospels, John and his readers would likely have been familiar with this anointing story.[44] Ridderbos writes, "The account here [John] bears a strong resemblance in outline and in certain details to the Markan account. Nowhere else is it more clear than precisely in these details that the Evangelist depended for his story on a more or less fixed tradition."[45] There are several similarities,[46] which would lead one to think John, at the very least, read Mark and would be familiar with the writer of Mark's use of intercalation.[47] Both John 12:1 and Mark 14:1 reference the Passover and both John 12:9 and Mark 14:10 introduce a new character once the inner story returns (John: large crowd of Jews; Mark: Judas). Both pericopes reference a dinner at a home (John 12:2; Mark 14:3); reveal that guests are present (John 12:1–2; Mark 14:3–4); mention a woman with a jar of pure nard (John 12:3; Mark 14:3); have a woman anointing Jesus (John 12:3; Mark 14:3); express disapproval at the expense of the nard being used (John 12:4–5; Mark 14:4–5); state that the perfume is valuable and the worth of the perfume should have been used for the poor (John 12:5; Mark 14:5); have Jesus defending the use of the perfume on himself (John 12:7–8; Mark 14:6–7); reference Jesus saying that they will always have the poor but not always have me (John 12:8; Mark 14:7).

The readers would also likely be familiar with the message of the anointing scene: preparation for Jesus's death and burial. Mark 14:8 and John 12:7 are the only New Testament occurrences for evntafiasmo,j

---

dated no later than the 40s (AD) while most acknowledge that John's Gospel was written around AD 90.

44. Kurek-Choycz, *Fragrance*, 351, writes: "The major differences between John and Mark can be explained either on the grounds of the redactional features characteristic for him, or as due to his reliance on Luke. The objections voiced by its critics, on the other hand, are not substantial enough. Rather than assume the existence of hypothetical sources for John 12:1–8, it is more plausible to presuppose that John's sources were the Synoptic Gospels."

45. Ridderbos, *Gospel according to John*, 412, brackets mine. Ridderbos goes on to compare John 12:3 with Mark 14:3 (and Matt 26:7), John 12:5 with Mark 14:5 and John 12:8 with Mark 14:8 in n99.

46. A good discussion on the differences of the Markan and Johannine anointing pericopes is in Carson, *Gospel according to John*, 426–27, who writes, "Apart from a number of details, none of which provides the remotest hint of contradiction. . . . In short, it is reasonable to suppose that what actually happened was comprehensive enough to generate the accounts of both John and Matthew/Mark, including the divergences that initially seem so odd."

47. Carson, *Gospel according to John*, 51.

meaning burial or preparation for burial.[48] With this in mind, injecting a familiar story of Jesus's anointing and using similar images as Mark's could trigger the reader of John to associate the pericope of Lazarus with the motif of death, burial, and preparation for burial based on reader familiarity.

Mark 14:1–11 as an Intercalation

John has already signaled the association of Mary's anointing with Lazarus's death in the previous chapter when John 11:2 interjects Mary anointing Jesus and wiping his feet with her hair with the fact that Lazarus was ill and would eventually die (John 11:2–11). If John is using Mark, then the writer would be familiar with Mark 14:1–11 also being an intercalation with the anointing sandwiched amid a death plot between the Jewish leaders and Judas.[49] The pericope of John 12:1–11 also has a "death plot," but instead of focusing on Jesus, Lazarus is now the object.

CONCLUSION

The anointing passages of John and Mark share common ground; there is evidence that John was familiar with the Markan anointing passage and familiar with Mark's usage of intercalation. Comparing the characteristics of John 12:1–11 with characteristics gleaned from the Markan intercalations, there is evidence that the Johannine pericope also employs this literary device. With a clear break away of Lazarus from John 12:1–2, no mention of Lazarus in 12:3–8, then reentering in John 12:9–11, the writer of John was using the familiar scene of Jesus's anointing to help communicate the circumstances Lazarus would face.

---

48. Matthew uses the verbal form evntafia,z, which means preparing for burial.

49. See also Edwards, "Markan Sandwiches," 208–9; Suggit, "Incident from Mark's Gospel"; Boring, *Mark*, 155–57, 379. Malick, "Examination of Jesus' View of Women," 7–8; Shepherd, *Markan Sandwich*, 243–50.

Appendix 2

The Curse of the Fig Tree Scene in Mark 11:14 and Jewish Observances

Abstract: The cursing of the fig tree scene in Mark 11:14 has been hermeneutically perplexing. Jesus's punitive act against a fig tree leads some to question the scene's historicity and depiction of Jesus's character. Many state that the section is communicating judgment as part of the larger pericope of Mark 11:12–25, but this solution has not appeased all. Studying Jewish observances—like Tisha B'Av and the Fifteenth of Sh'vat—could offer a better understanding of the fig tree cursing scene while helping to ameliorate the issues of historicity and the apparent inconsistent portrayal of Jesus.

Key Words: Fig Tree Curse, Tisha B'Av, Sh'vat/15th of Av, Jewish Observances, Jeremiah 8:13, Mark 11:14, judgment, Israel, temple.

FEW PERICOPES IN THE New Testament possess the plethora of perplexities as Mark 11:12–25. Stein postures nearly twenty hermeneutical concerns.[1] Kirk writes, "The scholarly literature on Mark 11:12–25 is rife with attempts to make sense of its numerous enigmas, and it is replete with pronouncements that such sense is not to be had."[2]

One issue in Mark 11:12–25 that has been puzzling to understand is Jesus's remark in Mark 11:14: "May no one ever eat fruit from you again,"[3] directed not toward a person, spirit, or creature, but a tree, appearing

---

1. Stein, *Mark*, 508–9.
2. Kirk, *Houses of Prayer*, 509.
3. In Mark 11:14, the verb φάγοι is one of the very rare occurrences of ἐσθίω in the optative mood which would signal to the reader, in addition to Mark 11:20–21, a cursing. See Lee, *Speech*, 13–15. The verb is not present in Matt 21:19.

Appendix 2

incongruent with Jesus's personality.[4] Later in Mark 11:20–21, the tree is described as "withered to its roots" and "cursed," adding to Jesus appearing overly punishing in Mark 11:14.

Critics of Mark's cursing scene are not sedate about their disapproval: "Mark's account of the cursing of the fig tree is much like a chronic disorder: the patient is always on treatment but never really cured."[5] "Certainly one of Jesus's most enigmatic and, to many readers, offensive actions."[6] "It is hard to imagine why Jesus should have misused his miraculous power in this petty way, and still harder to understand why anyone should record it.... It should have been possible to find a more wholesome narrative basis."[7]

Telford believes this scene was so vindictive that Luke deliberately omitted it.[8] The scene is even more disturbing when adding the Mark 11:13 phrase: "it was not the season for figs." This expression coupled with Mark 11:14 makes Jesus appear to be lashing out in anger due to hunger while possessing full knowledge of the tree's inability to satiate.[9] This leads some to question its historicity,[10] like Esler, who writes, "Mark found the

---

4. See Keener, *Commentary on the Gospel of Matthew*, 503. On the issue of the pericope and redaction criticism, see Esler, *Withered Fig*, 41–67; Telford, *Temple and Tree*; Kirk, *Houses of Prayer*, 509–13.

5. Cotter, "For It Was Not the Season," 62.

6. Hiers, "Not the Season for Figs," 394.

7. France, *Gospel of Mark*, 439 who later states that Matthew and Mark are able to teach the aspect of judgment in a more wholesome manner later in their writings. See also Manson, *Cleansing the Temple*, 259. Carson, *Matthew*, 446, argues that Jesus casting the demons into the swine supports the cursing of the fig tree scene as "not so far out of character." Carson writes, "Perhaps the fact that the two punitive miracles—the swine and the fig tree—are not directed against men should teach us something of Jesus's compassion."

8. Telford, *Temple and Tree*, 239, writes, "The harsh import of Mark's story was recognized by Luke who decided to omit it. The third evangelist replaced the pericope with a characteristic lament for Jerusalem and earlier has Jesus recount a parable of a barren fig-tree to which a period of grace was granted." See also Carson, *Matthew*, 444, for his critique of Telford.

9. See Hiers, "Not the Season for Figs," 394–400. Culpepper, *Mark*, 373, adds: "The most problematic aspect of this already difficult passage is Mark's comment that it was not time for figs." See also Kirk, *Houses of Prayer*, 520–22.

10. See Nolland, *Commentary on the Gospel of Luke*, 836. But Evans, *Mark*, 166, argues that most scholars adhere to the historicity of the text. Hiers, "Not the Season for Figs," 394, writes, "Interpreters have two main courses.... One is to suggest that somebody tampered with the text. The other is to propose a 'symbolic' explanation."

The Curse of the Fig Tree Scene in Mark 11:14

admittedly enigmatic story of Jesus cursing a fig tree in a source and felt compelled to make use of it as best he could."[11]

Many appeal to theological teaching in exonerating Jesus's behavior like Garland who references Mark's use of intercalation[12] in Jesus's exemption: "Mark's bracketing technique offers a solution to this puzzle and corrects any view that Jesus succumbs to a fit of irrational temper."[13] Or Stein who absolves by writing:

> The response of Jesus in 11:14 is not in any sense described as irate. Nothing is said of Jesus's emotional condition (contrast 1:43), and the description of Jesus's "cursing" the fig tree loses much of its supposed vitriolic flavor when we realize that this "cursing" has nothing to do with profanity and obscenity but refers rather to a symbolic act of condemnation and judgment.[14]

Stein goes on to write, "It is clear that Mark does not want his readers to think that what Jesus does in 11:14 is due to anger or rage."[15]

Nevertheless, the tone of Mark 11:14 appear atypical even if theological thinking is the motive. Though pointing to judgment quenches some dissonance, the critics' words still ring true: Mark could have found a more wholesome way to teach these lessons in which he clearly does in later chapters.[16]

One area that may help in reducing the severity of Mark 11:14 is adding an understanding of Jewish observances—for example, the Fast of Tisha B'Av[17] and Sh'vat/15th of Av[18]—to postulate if it is plausible for

---

11. Esler, *Withered Fig*, 62. See also Schwartz, *Der verfluchte Feigenbaum*, 80–84, on the withered tree as a legend of a tree that actually was on the road from Bethany to Jerusalem.

12. Garland uses the term bracketing for intercalation.

13. Garland, *Mark*, 433. Collins and Attridge, *Mark*, 525, state, "Critics should be cautious about exaggerating the degree to which the intercalated stories are intended to interpret one another." See also Kirk, *Houses of Prayer*, 511–12.

14. Stein, *Mark*, 513.

15. Ibid., 514. For a thorough discussion of the various interpretations, see Telford, *Temple and Tree*, 1–25, and Collins and Attridge, *Mark*, 522–37. On the issue of the fig tree scene teaching about believing prayer, see Carson, *Matthew*, 446. Stein, *Mark*, 508–9, 519, does not think Mark originally connected the cursing of the fig tree with believing prayer, see also Hooker, *Mark*, 269. Gundry, *Mark*, 650, also does not see the scene as shocking.

16. See France, *Gospel of Mark*, 439.

17. Also can be written as Tishoh B'Ov, Tishah Be-Av, Tisha B'Ab, and Ninth of Av/Ab.

18. Also known by names like 15 Shvat, Tu Bishvat, Tu B'Av, and Tu B'shvat.

them to be part of the verse's background. It has already been mentioned that Jesus's teaching on judgment brings absolution to some, I will further discuss this element of Mark 11:14 being part of this larger pericope which many consider corresponds to the coming judgment of the temple and Israel followed by a discussion of the Jewish holidays/fast of Tisha B'Av and Sh'vat/15th of Av to see if the option exists that Jewish remembrances could be an impetus behind the cursing of the fig tree scene.

Coming Judgment on Israel, Destruction of Temple

As mentioned above, many consider judgment the main topic of Mark 11:12–25, specifically of Israel and the temple. Mark 11:15–19—Jesus cleansing the temple— is inserted within the overall pericope of Mark 11:12–25 pointing to the fact that a coming judgment on the nation of Israel and/or the destruction of the temple will occur.[19] Boring writes, "That no one is to eat fruit from it forever shows that the pronouncement represents the ultimate, eschatological judgment of God . . . the withering tree from the roots up (v. 20) shows the utter devastation of the tree, which, representing the temple, is destroyed and will not recover."[20] Edwards writes, "The earliest commentary on the Gospel of Mark by Victor of Antioch in the fifth century already understood the event as an enactment parable in which the cursing of the fig tree symbolized the judgment to befall Jerusalem."[21] Telford writes, "Mark's readers . . . would readily have understood Jesus's cursing of the barren fig-tree as at the very least a judgment upon Israel."[22]

Though differing interpretations exists,[23] the dominant view throughout the discussions can be construed as the motif of judgment upon the nation and/or its temple. Because of the nature of the pericope, when the harshness of Mark 11:14 is attempted to be solved, the major topic cited is judgment, but as mentioned above, pointing to judgment does not satisfy some of the critics which leads to questioning the verse's historicity and

---

19. Some like Stein, *Mark*, 508–9, 519, see the cursing scene as originally unrelated to 11:22–25. Others like Esler, *Withered Fig*, 41–67, sees the pericope focused on faith and prayer.

20. Boring, *Mark*, 2006, 319.

21. Edwards, *Gospel according to Mark*, 339. Kirk, *Houses of Prayer*, 520.

22. Telford, *Temple and Tree*, 136. Also, Hooker, *Mark*, 261 writes, "The fig tree represents Israel, which has failed to produce the appropriate fruits when her Messiah looked for them."

23. See Telford, *Temple and Tree*, 1–25, and Collins and Attridge, *Mark*, 522–37.

Jesus's portrayal. Studying Jewish observances could help lessen some of the verse's severity.

Old Testament Background and Tisha B'Av

Relating the Old Testament to the cursing scene is common. The primary passages as listed by Telford are: Jer 8:13; Isa 28:3–4; Hos 9:10, 16; Mic 7:1; and Joel 1:7, 12.[24] Of these passages, Jer 8:13 has similarities with Mark 11:14, both contain themes of judgment while using corresponding terms and phrases—"no figs," "fig tree," and "wither"—which some see linking the two. Bas M. F. van Iersel writes, "The curse would answer perfectly what Jeremiah says about the inhabitants of Jerusalem: 'When I wanted to gather them, says the Lord, there are no grapes on the vine, nor figs on the fig tree (Jer. 8.13).'"[25] Witherington writes, "Now it is a subtle thing because at this juncture Jer. 8:13 is not cited at all, but surely it must be in the background."[26] Marshall believes Mark's audience would have connected Jesus's cursing with Jer 8:13: "The symbolism and dramatic impact of the story would certainly not have escaped Mark's original audience."[27] Collins writes, "Allusion may also be made to Jer. 8:13, which occurs in the context of an indictment of the leaders of the people (8:8–13)."[28]

Hays writes,

> The story of the withered fig tree explicitly echoes the judgment oracle found in Jeremiah 8:13. . . . Just as Jeremiah had spoken of

---

24. Telford, *Temple and Tree*, 142. One can also list such verses as Hab 3:17 and Jer 5:17.

25. Iersel, *Mark*, 357.

26. Witherington, *Gospel of Mark*, 312.

27. Marshall, *Faith as a Theme*, 160, see n3 for OT text references. He incorrectly writes Jer 8:12 instead of 8:13 and also associates with Isa 28:3f.; Mic 7:1; Joel 1:7, 12; and Hos 9:15f. See also Hooker, *Mark*, 261, where various OT passages are cited but the one that stands out is Jer 8:13.

28. Collins and Attridge, *Mark*, 525n28. But we will see later, not only can the pericope of 8:8–13 be cited but the larger pericope of 8:13—9:23 may be a better starting point. See also Gray, *Temple in the Gospel of Mark*, 35, who writes, "The withered fig tree . . . may be an allusion to Jeremiah 8:13." On the issue of Jer 7 being the basis for Jesus's action in the temple, see Horsley, *Hearing the Whole Story*, 110. On the issue of the Hebrew grammar, see Plaut, *Haftarah*, 749, who writes, "The Hebrew is difficult, and it has been suggested that a change of vocalization would make the phrase into the perfect parallel to what follows." Hooker, *Mark*, 267, states the original event would have its background in Aramaic which would be closer to Hebrew than the Koine Greek of the New Testament.

Israel as an unfruitful, withered fig tree, Jesus performs a symbolic tree-withering act that prefigures the fate of Israel—or, at least, of the Temple. . . . Jesus takes up the mantle of Jeremiah to condemn the Temple establishment once again. . . . As judgment fell upon Israel in Jeremiah's time, so it looms once again over the Temple.[29]

With Mark referencing figs, withering, and trees coupled with knowledge of Jeremiah, the prophet's rendition may have influenced Mark's cursing scene. But Jeremiah's words may not be the only influence; the prophet's words are read during the fast of Tisha B'Av.

Tisha B'Av

As noted above, the reference to figs, fig tree and withering would lead some to link Jer 8:13 with Mark 11:14, but the Jeremiah verse belongs to larger section that extends through 9:23, which happens to be read on the Jewish fast day of Tisha B'Av. Why would this be significant and relevant to the fig tree scene? The fast's dominant motif is the destruction of the temple, the subject many scholars believe is behind Jesus cursing the fig tree. Plaut writes,

> Tisha B'Av commemorates the tragedy of the Jewish people: the expulsion from its homeland and its subsequent exile. The Haftarah brings us the dark vision of Jeremiah, who later on was destined to witness the destruction and its terrible aftermath. "No selection for this day could have been more appropriate than the one before us."[30]

On the day of the fast, the whole book of Lamentations is read and the corresponding reading from the Haftarah (Prophets) is Jer 8:13—9:23. A form of this lectionary may have been present during Jesus's time.[31]

---

29. Hays, *Reading Backwards*, 8–9.
30. Plaut, *Haftarah*, 747.
31. Another issue that needs to be mentioned is whether or not the Jewish lectionary had any influence during New Testament times. The position of the NT being influenced by Jewish lectionaries was proposed by some like: Guilding, *Fourth Gospel*; Cave, *St. Matthew's Infancy*, 382–90, and Smith, *Tabernacles*, 130–46. For a response, see Morris, *New Testament and the Jewish Lectionaries*. Most recently, Gabriella Gelardini, in *Hebrews*, 110–11, writes, "The reading pairs were organized in lectionary cycles; we know of the existence of two such cycles, the Palestinian Triennial Cycle (PTC) and the Babylonian Annual Cycle (BAC). . . . The PTC . . . had been adapted by the ancient Romans Jewish community . . . the readings from the . . . Prophets no later than the first century CE, and

There are four fasts that commemorate the destruction of the temple but the most important of the four is Tisha B'Av. Schauss writes, "Tishoh B'Ov [Tish B'Av] . . . is a day of mourning, during which Jews fast and bewail the destruction of the Temple and Jerusalem."[32] Strassfeld writes, "The ninth of Av stands out from the other three fasts. . . . Tisha be-Av is so important because it marks the day when both temples were destroyed. . . . It is a major fast day and therefore bears some resemblance to the only other one in the Jewish calendar, Yom Kippur."[33] With many pointing to the Mark 11 pericope teaching an aspect of temple destruction and the major Jewish fast of Tisha B'Av commemorating temple destruction, there could be an association. One must ask if it is plausible that Tisha B'Av was celebrated during Jesus's time and if it possessed an agricultural aspect that might lead to the fig tree curse.

There is evidence that the fast may have been instituted in Zech 7:4–5; 8:19 labeled as the fast of the fifth month and was first enacted during the period of the second temple. Bloch writes,

> A messenger bearing the news of the capture of Jerusalem came to Ezekiel of the fifth of Tevet, 585 B.C.E., six months after the disaster (Ezek. 33:21). The news of the burning of the Temple must have reached the prophet soon thereafter, and the fast was most likely decreed on the first anniversary. This is substantiated by the words of Zechariah addressed to the Babylonian Jewish emissaries in the year 518 B.C.E.: "When you fasted and you mourned in the fifth and in the seventh month, almost these seventy years" (7:5). This statement made sixty-eight years after the destruction of the Temple, clearly indicates that the fast had been decreed shortly after the destruction of the Temple.[34]

Schauss writes, "Beginning with the Babylonian exile . . . there were certain days in the year which were ordained as national days of mourning

---

that the PTC was followed prior to the Second Temple's destruction." Gelardini goes on to argue on pp. 120–23 that the lectionary from the Palestinian Triennial Cycle is the basis for Hebrews and also argues on p. 125 that "the reconstruction readings are part of the PTC in early form, and they hint at the most important day of fasting in Jewish tradition, Tisha be-Av. This suggestion is confirmed when the central quotations and the theological concepts in Hebrews are compared with extra-biblical information on Tisha-be-Av."

32. Schauss, *Jewish Festivals*, 96.
33. Strassfeld, *Jewish Holidays*, 87.
34. Bloch, *Holy Days*, 247.

for all Jews.... These were all days of mourning connected with events at the time of destruction."³⁵

From this discussion, it is possible that Tisha B'Av could have been celebrated during the time of Christ and when Jesus curses the fig tree, the disciples who hear Christ's pronouncement (καὶ ἤκουον οἱ μαθηταὶ αὐτοῦ) may have associated it with the Jewish fast which commemorates the destruction of the temple.³⁶ We know from passages like Luke 4:17–19 that the Old Testament prophets were read in public and on Tisha B'Av, the Jeremiah pericope may have been read. But there are other passages in the Old Testament and other holidays that point to temple destruction and judgment; we must see if an agricultural dimension exists with Tisha B'Av and if it is possible this could influence the cursing scene.

Tisha B'Av, the Fifteenth of Sh'vat, and Trees

Studying Jewish observances, one does find that there is a "tree" aspect of the fast of Tisha B'Av, which occurs six days before the fifteenth of Sh'vat, the holiday observing trees. Trepp writes, "We cannot exclude the possibility that even this day [Tisha B'Av] may have connections with nature rites.... We shall find that the fifteenth of Av was observed as the feast of the tree harvest; it may well have been preceded by purging."³⁷ Trepp goes on to write, "As a day of purification preceding the tree harvest, Tishah b'Av would then correspond to the tenth of Tevet, the fast preceding the fifteenth of Sh'vat, New Year's Day of Trees, tree-planting time. One was observed as the days lengthened and nature awakened; the other, as the days grew shorter and nature had yielded its gifts."³⁸

When thinking of Jewish holidays and agriculture, the dominant three are: Passover, Shavout (Weeks or Pentecost), and Sukkot (Booths/Tabernacles) corresponding to harvests of barley, wheat, first fruits, and the

---

35. Schauss, *Jewish Festivals*, 98–99. Also, Strassfeld, *Jewish Holidays*, 87–88, states there may be a connection between Tisha B'Av and the twelve spies in Num 13; the midrash records "that God marked the ninth of Av as a day of catastrophe because of the incident of the spies in the desert... God then ordained the destruction of the temple on that day."

36. Many like Mary Healy, Healy and Williamson, *Mark*, 225, believe the reference to the disciples hearing the curse prepares the reader for the continuance of the story in Mark 11:20ff.

37. Trepp, *Jewish Observance*, 206, brackets mine.

38. Ibid., 206–7.

final celebration after all agriculture has been harvested, but many are not aware of the fifteenth of Sh'vat which has a connection with Tisha B'Av and a strong tree motif.[39] Trepp writes, "In Egypt, it was forbidden to injure any fruit trees because the god Osiris dwelt in them. We find a similar prohibition in Torah, which finds it necessary to reject any belief in a tree's human, much less divine, character, holding instead that a tree sustains life and is to be preserved even in warfare."[40] Trepp goes on to write,

> In joy, the awakening of the trees' life is observed. The fifteenth of Sh'vat is a pure festival of nature. . . . We are, however, bidden to partake of the fruit with which the land of Israel is especially blessed, for it is a land of wheat and barley, of vines, figs, and pomegranates, a land of olive and honey [Deut 8:8]. . . . The festival thus comes to reveal the significance of the restoration of Israel as a sovereign nation.[41]

The 15th of Av not only possesses a strong agricultural premise but also owns a national and temple motif. Bloch writes, "An examination of Talmudic sources . . . reveals four facets of the festival: (1) an agricultural holiday, (2) a matrimonial holiday for youth, (3) a temple holiday, (4) a national holiday."[42] Bloch goes on to write, "When the fifteenth of Av was reinstated in the Second Commonwealth as a festive day, it was no longer a youth festival but a Temple holiday."[43]

The fifteenth of Av was often celebrated in order to counter the grim mourning of the temple destruction of Tisha B'Av; Bloch writes, "The observance of a prolonged period of sorrow and mourning, culminating on Tisha B'Av, required a balancing day of joy to offset the sadness and to reassert Jewish hope and faith in a brighter future."[44] With the 15th of Av possessing a theme of trees, temple, and nation coupled with Tisha B'Av—the major day of mourning with temple destruction as its main facet—Mark may have been drawing on these observances to assist in his teaching.

---

39. Ibid., 153.

40. Ibid.

41. Ibid., 154. The fruit and grains mentioned in Deut 8:8 represent "the fertility of the land of Israel" in Greenberg, *Jewish Way*, 419. See also Greenberg, *Jewish Way*, 418, on the agricultural aspect of the holiday.

42. Bloch, *Holy Days*, 215.

43. Ibid., 217.

44. Ibid., 218.

Since the fig tree was withered to its roots instead of restored, could this communicate that there will be no rebirth, New Year, only total destruction of the temple? Since the 15th of Av followed Tisha B'Av appearing to balance Tisha B'Av's grimness, could Jesus be using the cursing scene to describe how the 15th of Av will not counter the mourning of Tisha B'Av and the temple will be destroyed once and for all while the nation will experience judgment? If the 15th of Av was celebrated during Jesus's time possessing such a strong tree motif, would the disciples associate its withering with the 15th of Av and have an idea of the coming judgment on the temple as well as national calamity? Both Jewish observances carried a temple motif and appeared to be associated with one another.

Conclusion

The cursing of the fig tree has caused emotional and hermeneutical havoc. From strong demonstrative responses to historicity issues, selected critics have not been appeased by efforts to exonerate Jesus's words. With Mark stating that Jesus's disciples heard his words of cursing (καὶ ἤκουον οἱ μαθηταὶ αὐτοῦ), Jesus had a much higher agenda than thrashing out his anger due to the tree's inability to appease his hunger. A strong point about the coming destruction of the temple and judgment on the nation could be the motive for the twelve to witness such a scene. With Tisha B'Av being the main fast mourning the destruction of the temple connected to the fifteenth of Av, which possesses aspects of the temple, trees, and national restoration, the disciples witnessing this act may associate the Jewish observances with teaching on coming judgment. Jesus's curse would be a strong object lesson on the coming catastrophe facing the temple and Israel based on entities that would be ingrained in Jewish culture and provide background that could assuage what appears to be an inconsistent portrayal of Jesus.

Bibliography

Baban, O. D. *On the Road Encounters in Luke-Acts: Hellenistic Mimesis and Luke's Theology of the Way*. Milton Keynes, UK: Paternoster, 2006.
Barnett, Paul. *Jesus and the Logic of History*. Grand Rapids: Eerdmans, 1997.
Barrett, C. K. *The Gospel according to St. John: An Introduction with Commentary and Notes on the Greek Text*. Philadelphia: Westminster, 1978.
Barth, M. *Rediscovering the Lord's Supper*. Eugene: Wipf & Stock, 1996.
Bauckham, Richard. *Jesus and the Eyewitnesses: The Gospels as Eyewitness Testimony*. Cambridge: Eerdmans, 2006.
———. "John for Readers of Mark." In *The Gospels for All Christians: Rethinking the Gospel Audiences*, edited by Richard Bauckham, 147–71. Grand Rapids: Eerdmans, 1998.
Beasley-Murray, G. R. *John*. 2nd ed. Word Bible Commentary. Nashville: Nelson, 1999.
Beavis, M. A. *Mark*. Paideia. Grand Rapids: Baker Academic, 2011.
Bell, D., and G. Valentine. *Consuming Geographies: We Are What We Eat*. London: Routledge, 1997.
Belle, Gilbert van. "Tradition, Exegetical Formation, and the Leuven Hypothesis." In *What We Have Heard from the Beginning*, edited by Tom Thatcher, 325–27. Waco: Baylor University Press, 2007.
Bloch, A. P. *The Biblical and Historical Background of the Jewish Holy Days*. New York: Ktav, 1978.
Blomberg, Craig L. *Contagious Holiness: Jesus' Meals with Sinners*. Downers Grove: InterVarsity, 2006.
———. *The Historical Reliability of John's Gospel*. Downers Grove: InterVarsity, 2011.
———. *The Historical Reliability of the Gospels*. 2nd ed. Downers Grove: IVP Academic, 2007.
Bock, D. *Luke*. Vol. 2, *9:51—24:53*. Baker Exegetical Commentary on the New Testament. Grand Rapids: Baker, 1996.
Boring, M. E. *Mark: A Commentary*. New Testament Library. Louisville: Westminster John Knox, 2006.
Brown, B. *Daring Greatly: How the Courage to Be Vulnerable Transforms the Way We Live, Love, Parent, and Lead*. New York: Gotham, 2012.
———. *The Gifts of Imperfection: Let Go of Who You Think You're Supposed to Be and Embrace Who You Are*. Center City, MN: Hazelden, 2010.
Brown, R. E. *The Death of the Messiah: From Gethsemane to the Grave; A Commentary on the Passion Narratives in the Four Gospels*. New York: Doubleday, 1994.
———. *The Gospel according to John*. 2 vols. Garden City: Doubleday, 1966.
Brown, Scott G. "Mark 11:1—12:12: A Triple Intercalation?" *Catholic Biblical Quarterly* 64 (2002) 78.

Bibliography

Burge, G. M. *John: From Biblical Text . . . to Contemporary Life*. Grand Rapids: Zondervan, 2000.
Byrne, B. *Lazarus: A Contemporary Reading of John 11:1-46*. Homebush, Australia: St. Paul, 1991.
Carson, D. A. *The Gospel according to John*. Grand Rapids: Eerdmans, 1991.
———. *Matthew*. Expositor's Bible Commentary. Grand Rapids: Zondervan, 1984.
Cave, C. H. "St. Matthew's Infancy Narrative." *New Testament Studies* 9 (1963) 382-90.
Chapple, Allan. "Jesus' Intervention in the Temple: Once or Twice?" *Journal of the Evangelical Theological Society* 58 (2011) 545-69.
Chester, T. *A Meal with Jesus: Discovering Grace, Community, and Mission around the Table*. Wheaton: Crossway, 2011.
Cloud, H, and J. S. Townsend. *Boundaries*. Dvd. Grand Rapids: Zondervan, 2007.
Coakley, J. F. "The Anointing at Bethany and the Priority of John." *Journal of Biblical Literature* 107 (1988) 241-56.
Collins, A. Y., and H. W. Attridge. *Mark: A Commentary*. Hermeneia. Minneapolis: Fortress, 2007.
Cotter, W. J. "For It Was Not the Season for Figs." *Catholic Biblical Quarterly* 48 (1986) 62-66.
Craddock, Fred B. *Luke*. Louisville: John Knox, 1990.
Culpepper, R. A. *The Gospel and Letters of John*. Nashville: Abingdon, 1998.
———. *Mark*. Smith & Helwys Bible Commentary. Macon, GA: Smyth and Helwys, 2007.
Davies, W. D., and D. C. Allison. *A Critical and Exegetical Commentary on the Gospel according to Saint Matthew*. Vol. 3, *XIX-XXVIII*. Edinburgh: T. & T. Clark, 1997.
Dearman, J. Andrew *Jeremiah, Lamentations*. Grand Rapids: Zondervan, 2002.
Delobel, J. "L'onction par la pécheresse: La composition littéraire de Lc. VII, 36-50." *Ephemerides Theologicae Lovanienses* 42 (1966) 415-75.
Demir, M., et al. "Friendship and Happiness." In *The Oxford Handbook of Happiness*, edited by F. E. Gaebelein, 860-72. Oxford: Oxford University Press, 2013.
Dobschütz, Ernst von. "Zur Erzählerkunst des Markus." *Zeitschrift für die neutestamentliche Wissenschaft* 27 (1928) 193-98.
Dodd, C. H. *Historical Tradition in the Fourth Gospel*. Cambridge: Cambridge University Press, 1963.
Donahue, John R., and Daniel J. Harrington. *The Gospel of Mark*. Collegeville: Liturgical, 2002.
Downing, F. Gerald. "Markan Intercalation in Cultural Context." In *Nativity in Biblical and Related Texts*, edited by G. J. Brooke and J. D. Kaestli, 105-18. Leuven: Leuven University Press, 2000.
Duke, P. D. *Irony in the Fourth Gospel*. Atlanta: John Knox, 1985.
Edwards, J. R. *The Gospel according to Mark*. Grand Rapids: Eerdmans, 2002.
———. "Markan Sandwiches: The Significance of Interpolations in Markan Narratives." *Novum Testamentum* 31 (1989) 197.
Elliott, J. K. "The Anointing of Jesus." *Expository Times* 85 (1974) 105-7.
Esler, P. F. "The Incident of the Withered Fig Tree in Mark 11: A New Source and Redactional Explanation." *Journal for the Study of the New Testament* 28 (2005) 41-67.
Esler, P. F., and R. A. Piper. *Lazarus, Mary and Martha: A Social-Scientific and Theological Reading of John*. London: SCM, 2006.
Evans, C. A. *Mark 8:27—16:20*. Word Biblical Commentary. Nashville: Nelson, 2001.

BIBLIOGRAPHY

Fortna, R. T. *The Gospel of Signs*. Society for New Testament Studies Monograph Series. Cambridge: University Press, 1970.

France, R. T. *The Gospel of Mark: A Commentary on the Greek Text*. Grand Rapids: Eerdmans, 2002.

———. *The Gospel of Matthew*. Grand Rapids: Eerdmans, 2007.

Gardner-Smith, P. *Saint John and the Synoptic Gospels*. Cambridge: Cambridge University Press, 1938.

Garland, D. E. *Mark: From Biblical Text to Contemporary Life*. NIV Application Commentary. Grand Rapids: Zondervan, 1996.

Gaultiere, B. "Jesus' Way of Dealing with Anger." SoulShepherding.org. July 23, 2012. http://www.soulshepherding.org/2012/07/jesus-way-of-dealing-with-anger.

Gelardini, G. "Hebrews, an Ancient Synagogue Homily for Tisha be-Av: Its Function, Its Basis, Its Theological Interpretation." In *Hebrews: Contemporary Methods—New Insights*, edited by G. Gelardini, 107–24. Leiden: Brill, 2005.

Gilmour, Michael J. "Delighting in the Sufferings of Others: Early Christian Schadenfreude and the Function of the Apocalypse of Peter." *Bulletin for Biblical Research* 16 (2006) 129–39.

Goodenough, E. R. "John a Primitive Gospel." *Journal of Biblical Literature* 64 (1945) 152–55.

Grabbe, L. L. *An Introduction to Second Temple Judaism: History and Religion of the Jews in the Time of Nehemiah, the Maccabees, Hillel, and Jesus*. London: T. & T. Clark, 2010.

Gray, T. C. *The Temple in the Gospel of Mark*. Grand Rapids: Baker Academic, 2008.

Green, J. B. *The Gospel of Luke*. Grand Rapids: Eerdmans, 1997.

Green, J. B., and H. E. Hearon. "Anointing." In *Dictionary of Jesus and the Gospels*, edited by J. B. Green et al., 13. Downers Grove: InterVarsity, 1992.

Greenberg, Rabbi Irving. *The Jewish Way: Living the Holidays*. New York: Touchstone, 1993.

Guilding, A. *The Fourth Gospel and Jewish Worship: A Study of the Relation of St. John's Gospel to the Ancient Jewish Lectionary System*. Oxford: Clarendon, 1960.

Gundry, R. H. *Mark: A Commentary on His Apology for the Cross*. Grand Rapids: Eerdmans, 1993.

Hamm, D. "The Talmid Service in Luke-Acts: The Cultic Background behind Luke's Theology of Worship." *Catholic Biblical Quarterly* 65 (2003) 215–31.

Hayes, E. "The Unity of the Egyptian Hallel: Psalms 113–18." *Bulletin for Biblical Research* 9 (1999) 145–56.

Hays, R. B. *Reading Backwards: Figural Christology and the Fourfold Gospel Witness*. Waco: Baylor University Press, 2014.

Healy, M., and P. S. Williamson. *The Gospel of Mark*. Grand Rapids: Baker Academic, 2008.

Hendricksen, W. *Exposition of the Gospel of Luke*. New Testament Commentary. 10th ed. Grand Rapids: Baker, 2002.

———. *Exposition of the Gospel Mark*. New Testament Commentary. Grand Rapids: Baker, 1975.

Heschel, A. J. *The Sabbath*. New York: Noonday, 1979.

Hiers, R. H. "Not the Season for Figs." *Journal of Biblical Literature* 87 (1968) 394–400.

Holst, R. "The One Anointing of Jesus: Another Application of the Form-Critical Method." *Journal of Biblical Literature* 95 (1976) 435–46.

Bibliography

Holt-Lunstad, J., et al. "Social Relationships and Mortality Risk: A Meta-analytic Review." *Medicine* 7 (2010). doi:10.1371/journal.pmed.1000316.

Hooker, M. D. *The Gospel according to St. Mark*. Peabody: Hendrickson, 1991.

———. *The Gospel according to Saint Mark*. Black's Commentaries on the New Testament. London: A&C Black, 1991.

Horsley, R. A. *Hearing the Whole Story: The Politics of Plot in Mark's Gospel*. Louisville: Westminster John Knox, 2011.

Howard, Wilbert Francis. *The Fourth Gospel in Recent Criticism and Interpretation*. 3rd ed. London: Epworth, 1945.

Iersel, B. M. *Mark: A Reader-Response Commentary*. Sheffield: Sheffield Academic, 1998.

Isaacs, R. H. "Shabbat HaGadol." MyJewishLearning.com. March 28, 2003. http://www.myjewishlearning.com/holidays/Jewish_Holidays/Passover/In_the_Community/Shabbat_HaGadol.shtml.

Jeremias, Joachim. *New Testament Theology: The Proclamation of Jesus*. New York: Scribner, 1971.

Kahn, A. "Shabbat HaGadol." Aish.com. M'oray Ha'Aish series. March 31, 2001. http://www.aish.com/tp/i/moha/48942426.html.

Karris, R. *Luke: Artist and Theologian*. Eugene: Wipf & Stock, 1985.

Keener, C. S. *A Commentary on the Gospel of Matthew*. Grand Rapids: Eerdmans, 1999.

———. *The Gospel of John*. 2 vols. Peabody: Hendrickson, 2003.

———. *The Historical Jesus of the Gospels*. Grand Rapids: Eerdmans, 2009.

Kelley, R. L. "Meals with Jesus in Luke's Gospel." *Horizons in Biblical Theology* 17 (1995) 123–31.

Kernaghan, R. J. *Mark*. Downers Grove: InterVarsity, 2007.

King, P. J. *Jeremiah: An Archaeological Companion*. Louisville: Westminster John Knox, 1993.

Kirk, J. R. "Time for Figs, Temple Destruction, and Houses of Prayer in Mark 11:12–25." *Catholic Biblical Quarterly* 74 (2012) 509–27.

Kittler, P. G., and K. Sucher. *Food and Culture in America*. New York: Van Rostrand Reinhold, 1989.

Kodell, J. *The Eucharist in the New Testament*. Wilmington, DE: Glazier, 1988.

Koperski, V. "Luke 10:38–42 and Acts 6:1–7: Women and Discipleship in the Literary Context of Luke-Acts." In *The Unity of Luke-Acts*, edited by J. Verheyden, 517–44. Leuven: Leuven University Press, 1999.

Köstenberger, A. J. *John*. Grand Rapids: Baker Academic, 2004.

Köstenberger, A. J., and J. Taylor. *The Final Days of Jesus: The Most Important Week of the Most Important Person Who Ever Lived*. Wheaton: Crossway, 2014.

Kurek-Chomycz, D. A. "The Fragrance of Her Perfume: The Significance of Sense Imagery in John's Account of the Anointing in Bethany." *Novum Testamentum* 52 (2010) 344–51.

Kushner, H. S. *When Bad Things Happen to Good People*. New York: Schocken, 1981.

Lee, J. A. "Some Features of the Speech of Jesus in Mark's Gospel." *Novum Testamentum* 27 (1985) 13–15.

Legault, A. "An Application of the Form-Critical Method to the Anointings in Galilee and Bethany." *Catholic Biblical Quarterly* 16 (1954) 131–45.

Lindars, B. *The Gospel of John*. New Century Bible Commentary. Grand Rapids: Eerdmans, 1972.

Bibliography

Lohmeyer, E. *Das Evangelium des Markus.* 17th ed. Göttingen: Vandenhoeck and Ruprecht, 1967.

Maccini, R. G. *Her Testimony Is True: Women as Witnesses according to John.* Journal for the Study of the New Testament Supplement. Sheffield: Sheffield Academic, 1996.

Magnes, J. L. *Sense and Absence: Structure and Suspension in the End of Mark's Gospel.* Atlanta: Scholars, 1986.

Malick, D. E. "An Examination of Jesus's View of Women through Three Intercalations in the Gospel of Mark." *Priscilla Papers* 27 (2013) 4–15.

Malina, B. J., and R. L. Rohrbaugh. *Social-Science Commentary on the Gospel of John.* Minneapolis: Fortress, 1998.

Manson, T. W. "The Cleansing of the Temple." *Bulletin of the John Rylands Library* 33 (1951) 259.

Marshall, C. D. *Faith as a Theme in Mark's Narrative.* Cambridge: Cambridge University Press, 1989.

März, C. P. "Zur Traditionsgeschichte von Mk 14,3–9 und Parallelen." *Studien zum Neuen Testament und seiner Umwelt* 6/7 (1981/82) 106–11.

Michaels, J. R. *The Gospel of John.* Grand Rapids: Eerdmans, 2010.

Moloney, F. J. *The Gospel of Mark: A Commentary.* Grand Rapids: Baker Academic, 2002.

Moloney, F. J., and D. J. Harrington. *The Gospel of John.* Collegeville: Liturgical, 1998.

Mora, E., and J. Lucas. "Hematidrosis: Blood Sweat." *Blood* 121 (2013) 1493. http://www.bloodjournal.org/content/121/9/1493?sso-checked=true.

Morris, L. *The Gospel according to John: The English Text with Introduction, Exposition and Notes.* Grand Rapids: Eerdmans, 1971.

———. *Luke.* 2nd ed. Downers Grove: InterVarsity, 1988.

———. *The New Testament and the Jewish Lectionaries.* London: Tyndale, 1964.

Moule, C. F. *The Gospel according to Mark.* Cambridge: Cambridge University Press, 1965.

Neyrey, J. H. "Ceremonies in Luke-Acts: The Case of Meals and Table Fellowship." In *The Social World of Luke-Acts: Models for Interpretation,* 361–87. Peabody: Hendrickson, 1991.

Nolland, J. *Commentary on the Gospel of Luke 1—9:20.* Word Biblical Commentary. Waco: Word, 1989.

———. *The Gospel of Matthew: A Commentary on the Greek Text.* New International Greek Testament Commentary. Grand Rapids: Eerdmans, 2005.

Oakman, D. E. "Cursing Fig Trees and Robbers' Dens: Pronouncement Stories with Social-Systemic Perspective: Mark 11:11–25 and Parallels." *Semeia* 64 (1993) 256–57.

Painter, J. *Mark's Gospel: Worlds in Conflict.* London: Routledge, 1997.

Palmer, C. "From Theory to Practice: Experiencing the Nation in Everyday Life." *Journal of Material Culture* 3 (1998) 194.

Pao, D. W. "Waiters or Preachers: Acts 6:1–7 and the Lukan Table Fellowship Motif." *Journal of Biblical Literature* 130 (2011) 127–44.

Pate, C. M. *The Writings of John: A Survey of the Gospel, Epistles, and Apocalypse.* Grand Rapids: Zondervan, 2011.

Plaut, W. G., et al. *The Haftarah Commentary.* New York: UAHC Press, 1996.

Powell, M. A. *Introducing the New Testament: A Historical, Literary, and Theological Survey.* Grand Rapids: Baker Academic, 2009.

Reinbold, W. *Der älteste Bericht über den Tod Jesu: Literarische Analyse und historische Kritik der Passionsdarstellungen der Evangelien.* Berlin: de Gruyter, 1994.

Rich, T. R. "Special Shabbatot." Judaism 101. http://www.jewfaq.org/special.htm.

BIBLIOGRAPHY

Ridderbos, H. N. *The Gospel according to John: A Theological Commentary*. Grand Rapids: Eerdmans, 1997.

Robbins, Vernon. "Summons and Outline in Mark: The Three-Step Progression." *Novum Testamentum* 23 (1981) 97–114.

Robinson, J. A. T. *The Priority of John*. London: SCM Press, 1985.

Rosik, M. "The Greek Motif of the Cyclic Journey in the Gospel of Luke." *Journal of Greco-Roman Christianity and Judaism* 5 (2008) 165–73.

Sabbe, M. "The Anointing of Jesus in John 12:1–8 and Its Synoptic Parallels." In *The Four Gospels, 1992: Festschrift Frans Neirynck*, edited by F. Neirynck and F. Van Segbroeck, 2051–82. 3 vols. Leuven: Leuven University Press / Peeters, 1992.

Sanders, E. P. *The Historical Figure of Jesus*. New York: Penguin, 1993.

Sanders, J. N. "Those Whom Jesus Loved (John xi.5)." *New Testament Studies* 1 (1954–55) 29–41.

Schauss, H. *The Jewish Festivals: A Guide to Their History and Observance*. New York: Schocken, 1996.

Schnackenburg, R. "Der johanneische Bericht von der Salbung in Bethanien (Joh. 12, 1–8)." *Münchener theologische Zeitschrift* 1 (1950) 48–52.

Schwartz, Eduard. "Der verfluchte Feigenbaum." *ZNW* 5 (1904) 80–84.

Schweizer, E. *Good News according to Mark*. Richmond: John Knox, 1970.

Seim, T. K. *The Double Message: Patterns of Gender in Luke-Acts*. Nashville: Abingdon, 1994.

Senior, Daniel. *The Passion of Jesus in the Gospel of John*. Collegeville: Liturgical, 1991.

Shepherd, T. *Markan Sandwich Stories: Narration, Definition, and Function*. Berrien Springs, MI: Andrews University Press, 1993.

Smith, C. W. "Tabernacles in the Fourth Gospel and Mark." *New Testament Studies* 9 (1963) 130–46.

Smith, D. E. "Table Fellowship as a Literary Motif in the Gospel of Luke." *Journal of Biblical Literature* 106 (1987) 613–38.

Smith, D. M. *John among the Gospels: The Relationship in Twentieth-Century Research*. Minneapolis: Fortress, 1992.

Smith, R. H. "The Tomb of Jesus." *Biblical Archaeology* 30 (1967) 74–89.

Stein, R. H. *Luke*. Baker Exegetical Commentary on the New Testament. New American Commentary. Nashville: Broadman, 1992.

———. *Mark*. Baker Exegetical Commentary on the New Testament. Grand Rapids: Baker Academic, 2008.

Strassfeld, M., et al. *The Jewish Holidays: A Guide and Commentary*. New York: Harper & Row, 1985.

Strauss, C. Levi. *The Raw and the Cooked*. London: Penguin, 1986.

Suggit, J. "An Incident from Mark's Gospel." *Journal of Theology South Africa* 50 (1985) 52–55.

Tannahill, R. *Food in History*. St. Albans: Paladin, 1975.

Taylor, V. *The Gospel according to Mark*. 2nd ed. London: Macmillan, 1966.

Telford, V. W. *The Barren Temple and the Withered Tree: A Redaction-Critical Analysis of the Cursing of the Fig-Tree Pericope in Mark's Gospel and Its Relation to the Cleansing of the Temple Tradition*. Sheffield: JSOT, 1980.

———. "More Fruit from the Withered Tree." *New Testament Studies* 48 (1981) 264–304.

Thomas, Heath, et al., eds. *Holy War in the Bible: Christian Morality and an Old Testament Problem*. Downers Grove: IVP Academic, 2013.

BIBLIOGRAPHY

Tite, Philip L. "Pax, Peace and the New Testament." *Religiologiques* 11 (1995) 301–24.
Trepp, L. *The Complete Book of Jewish Observance*. New York: Behrman/Summit, 1980.
Van Til, K. A. "Three Anointings and One Offering: The Sinful Woman in Luke 7.36–50." *Journal of Pentecostal Theology* 15 (2006) 73–82.
Vande Vrede, K. "A Contrast between Nicodemus and John the Baptist in the Gospel of John." *Journal of the Evangelical Theological Society* 57 (2014) 715–26.
Warren, Rick. *The Purpose Driven Life*. Grand Rapids: Zondervan, 2002.
Whitacre, R. A. *John*. Downers Grove: InterVarsity, 1999.
Wilkins, M. J. *Matthew: From Biblical Text . . . to Contemporary Life*. Grand Rapids: Zondervan, 2004.
Witherington, B. *The Gospel of Mark: A Socio-Rhetorical Commentary*. Grand Rapids: Eerdmans, 2001.
———. *John's Wisdom: A Commentary on the Fourth Gospel*. Louisville: Westminster John Knox, 1995.

www.ingramcontent.com/pod-product-compliance
Lightning Source LLC
Chambersburg PA
CBHW070923180426
43192CB00037B/1731